TEACHING YOUNG CHILDREN
IN VIOLENT TIMES

TEACHING YOUNG CHILDREN IN VIOLENT TIMES:

BUILDING
A
PEACEABLE
CLASSROOM

Diane E. Levin, Ph.D.

With Foreword by Deborah Prothrow-Stith, M.D.

esr

EDUCATORS
for
SOCIAL
RESPONSIBILITY

23 Garden Street
Cambridge, MA 02138
(617) 492-1764

Teaching Young Children in Violent Times: Building a Peaceable Classroom
by Diane E. Levin, Ph.D.

Editor: Laura Parker Roerden

Levin, Diane E.
ISBN 0-86571-316-2 (soft cover)
ISBN 0-86571-315-4 (hard cover)

Inquiries regarding permission to reprint all or part of *Teaching Young Children in Violent Times* should be addressed to: Educators for Social Responsibility, 23 Garden Street, Cambridge, MA 02138.

Permission is gratefully acknowledged to NAEYC and CEASE for the use of their position statements on violence.

A special thanks to Debra Poklemba-Anderson for the use of her puppet photos.

 This book is printed on recycled paper.

Cover and book design by Karla Tolbert
Copyeditor: David Reich
Production Editors: Jeremy Rehwaldt and Linda Hiltz
Production Assistant: Vicki Jenkins

Teaching Young Children in Violent Times is distributed to the trade through New Society Publishers, 4527 Springfield Avenue, Philadelphia, PA 19143 (800) 333-9093; (215) 382-6543 or P.O. Box 189, Gabriola Island, BC VOR IXO

Dedication

For my husband, Gary Goldstein,
and
my son, Eli Levin-Goldstein,
with love and thanks
for all you have taught me about
learning to live in a
"Peaceable Home."

TABLE OF CONTENTS

PART I

Establishing the Foundations for Peace

PART II

Practical Ideas for Teaching Peace

Classroom Discussions

Figures and Tables

Acknowledgements

Many people have contributed to the creation of this book. My deep appreciation and thanks go to:

- Karen Economopoulos, whose deep and unfailing respect for children and ground-breaking teaching contributed immeasurably to my understanding of Peaceable Classrooms and the ideas, conversations, and activities described here;

- William Kreidler, whose unique understanding of how to help young children learn to work out their conflicts peacefully and whose generosity in fully sharing that knowledge and skill with me contributed to a whole new direction in my work and, ultimately, to the need to write this book;

- Nancy Carlsson-Paige, whom I have known for over twenty years—first, as my student, then as my colleague, and then as my friend and collaborator in the writing of three books—and who helped me get to the point of being ready to write this book;

- Sue Kranz and Debra Poklemba-Anderson, committed and inspired teachers, who have contributed ideas presented here and whose Peaceable Classroom curriculum-building activities serve as a model for us all;

- many other teachers who, through their daily efforts to create safe, peaceful, and empowering classrooms for young children, helped me decide to write this book;

- the many, many children who taught me so much about learning to live peacefully in a violent world—by letting me watch them play, talk, try to work out their problems, and go about their daily efforts to grow and develop in positive ways; and who helped convince me not only that Peaceable Classrooms are possible but also that Peaceable Classrooms are what children seek;

- Liz Kinstlinger and Beth Thomas, graduate research assistants at Wheelock College, who helped me with many of the classroom examples presented here—collecting data, transcribing tapes, and assisting me with whatever peculiar task I might ask;

- Zell Draz, for her friendship, unfailing interest in this work, and very generous support;

- the Longview Foundation for Education in World Affairs and International Understanding and The Frances R. Dewing Foundation, which provided funding for this book, and The Peace Development Fund, which supported Nancy Carlsson-Paige's and my research on conflict resolution;

- Wheelock College, for providing an environment in which this work could grow and flourish;

- the many colleagues who have helped me understand and effectively respond to violence in children's lives, including the members of the Panel on Violence in the Lives of Children of the National Association for the Education of Young Children, the members of the Peaceable Schools Group in Cambridge, Massachusetts, and the staff at the Boston City Hospital Family Development Center;

- my reviewers, whose insightful feedback contributed a great deal to the book—Ruth Bowman, Helen Cohen, Karen Economopoulos, Winifred Feise, Lynne Hall, Susan Hopkins, Shirley Jenkins, Judith Kulczycki, Julie Mjos MacGregor, Patricia Hnatiuk, Sally Orme, Debra Poklemba-Anderson, Rebecca Wheat, and Sheli Wortis;

- my editors at Educators for Social Responsibility—first, Sonja Latimore, who asked me to write this book and participated in the open give-and-take dialogue that led to its conceptualization, and then Laura Parker Roerden, who gave this project her wholehearted support from the very first day she arrived on the job, without both of whom not only would this book not have been written, but it certainly would not have been the meaningful and rewarding experience it has become for me;

- and finally, my husband Gary, who has always truly valued my passion for doing this work and supported me in my efforts to do it in more ways than I could ever list here; and my son, Eli, who has kept me grounded in the realities of raising a child in this violent world and given me the need and desire to forge forever ahead with this work.

Foreword

Violence is one of the most pressing issues facing our nation. National surveys indicate that the majority of Americans think violence is our number one problem. Current efforts to respond focus mainly on catching and punishing the perpetrators of violence, yet this should not be our only focus. The prison population is growing at an incredible rate—from 315,000 in 1980 to over 925,000 today. Thirty-three billion dollars have been spent on building new prisons since 1985. Despite the massive infusion of money, the crime rate continues its rapid rise, especially among our youth.

As a physician, I am deeply frustrated and concerned by the absence of an effective national approach to escalating violence in our streets and homes. Building more prisons is not a long-term solution. Something is seriously wrong when we spend $18-20,000 per year to keep a person in jail and $1 million to put a teenager in jail for life, but are unwilling to invest in programs that prevent antisocial behavior. America can no longer afford to emphasize such expensive and short-sighted responses to this critical problem. The future rests on how we raise our children, and here is where we must focus far more of our efforts. More and more violence has become a legacy our kids inherit. It is time to bequeath them something more positive.

We must develop multifaceted solutions for dealing with violence. We need strategies that change attitudes about violence and teach alternatives to violent behavior. These approaches are more sensible and cost effective. They provide our best chance for breaking the current cycle of violence.

Education is one vital place where we must turn. The classroom offers a powerful environment for changing behaviors. Public health campaigns like anti-smoking and safety helmets have successfully reduced risky behavior. These efforts demonstrate that positive behaviors can be taught as effectively as negative ones if we decide to put resources and expertise into doing so.

Learning to get along without violence is a skill that should be taught at early ages, then reinforced and practiced throughout a lifetime. The more we practice, the better we get at this skill.

In *Teaching Young Children in Violent Times*, Diane Levin gives us hope. She shows the great impact we can have when our efforts to prevent violence begin with children when they are young—before they have learned to accept violence as a way of life and before their behavior has become a threat to society. It starts to address early on attitudes and behaviors about violence that need to be unlearned.

Diane's approach is both comprehensive and practical. First, she helps teachers understand the nature of the problem—how young children are surrounded by violence in many forms, from entertainment violence in the media to real violence in the home and community. Then, she paints a powerful and useful picture of the many ways children are being affected by that violence. Once this foundation has been laid, Diane helps us understand the vital role teachers can play in counteracting those effects by creating what she calls a Peaceable Classroom. Diane also offers many innovative and comprehensive strategies for helping young children learn alternatives to the violent behaviors that are so often modeled for them in society. By so doing, she shows us how to teach young children to develop the understanding and skill they need for living peacefully with others.

This book will help many teachers feel ready and able to take on the challenge of effectively *Teaching Young Children in Violent Times*. Diane Levin provides a crucial piece of the solution that is needed to create a comprehensive and effective response to violence in society.

Teaching Young Children in Violent Times is an important resource for anyone concerned with our society's violence. Teachers, school administrators, policymakers, and parents will find this a greatly informative book.

DEBORAH PROTHROW-STITH, M.D.

PART I

Establishing the Foundations for Peace

Introduction

FROM TURTLES TO DOVES: CHALLENGES OF TEACHING YOUNG CHILDREN IN VIOLENT TIMES

In the summer of 1967, I was in Detroit, Michigan, with a group of beginning early childhood teachers from all over the country. We were studying how President Johnson's War on Poverty was affecting children and families who were living in poverty in the inner city. Head Start, then in its infancy, offered new hope; it was part of a comprehensive set of programs and services to help "lift" children and families out of poverty. Government officials and human service providers alike were optimistic about the future. Detroit was described then as a "demonstration city" because it had quickly and effectively taken advantage of all available programs and resources provided by the federal government to fight the War on Poverty. The deterioration of inner city Detroit had been halted, and many in high places were hopeful that the trend had even been reversed.

Then, late one steamy summer night, I woke up to the smell of smoke. I looked out the window and saw the glow of flames in the distance. Then I heard sirens, many of them, even an occasional gunshot. Others awoke. We turned on the radio to learn that the city had erupted in violence.

The Detroit riot of 1967 had begun. Over the next few days we got a small taste of what it means to live in a war zone. We were housebound. Tanks and trucks filled with National Guardsmen in full army gear went by our windows. We heard regular sniper fire, as well as the return fire of the soldiers' machine guns. At night, we had to cover windows before turning on lights. We developed extensive procedures for evacuating the building in case of fire and for evacuating the city altogether. A few days later, we were taken on a tour to inspect the ashes and rubble.

Two years later, I had my first job, as a teacher/group therapist at a mental health center that treated emotionally disturbed young children. Many children who came to the center had been suspended from public school kindergartens for aggression and violence—what was then called antisocial behavior. Working with these children, who were so small and needy and yet so angry and hostile, was an enormous challenge. I had had special training, but it was not enough. Training could not have adequately prepared me to help these children overcome all of the factors that had led to their problems.

Often I empathized with these children's kindergarten teachers, who had thrown up their hands in despair and banished them. In fact, one day, at what was probably the low point of my work at the Center, I was actually physically attacked—first, by the smallest five-year-old in the group and then by several others who joined in. With the help of another teacher I managed to quell the disturbance. Fortunately, I was more shaken than injured. But many times since, I have thought about what might have happened if the other teacher had not been there.

Later, I went to several more experienced colleagues for support and supervision. We all expressed surprise, and even shock, that children so young could be so violent and out of control. We worked closely together to better understand the children and the attack and to strategize about how to help them heal while keeping ourselves and the other children safe.

The riots and my experience at the mental health center occurred about twenty-five years ago. The world has changed dramatically since then. Today, urban areas have continued to deteriorate. One child in five lives in poverty, a 21 percent increase since 1970.* The violence that grows out of poverty and economic injustice now touches the lives of many of us. And government efforts to stem the tide have shriveled, as has the promise that poverty and its effects can be eliminated by a few government programs.

Today, many of you, perhaps, are not surprised to hear of five- and six-year-old perpetrators or victims of violence. What was a rarity then, has become what can seem like an epidemic. And its effects are felt in many classrooms, though we may not even recognize it. I'm sure many of you can think of angry and aggressive children, like those who were suspended from kindergarten, who regularly try to hurt themselves and others. But getting them help at mental health centers is not often an option now, as services for children and families have been repeatedly slashed. And, even where such services still do exist, they would need to be expanded to make a dent in meeting the needs that currently exist. The special skills required for working with children around the issues of conflict and violence, which go beyond those of even the trained group therapist of twenty-five years ago, are now needed by many early childhood teachers as part of everyday classroom life.

In my current work, I spend a lot of time working with teachers and parents of young children around issues of violence and conflict. And recently, I began co-teaching a course called Violence in the Lives of Children and Families. In this work, I hear about the many ways violence is entering the

---

* "Report: US Lags on Child Health: Poorer Nations Making Strides," *Boston Globe*, 23 September 1993.

lives of children from all walks of life. I hear about children who do not know how to resolve their differences without resorting to fists. I listen to concerns about the impact on children of media and entertainment violence. I note the groans every time I am with a group of teachers and mention the Teenage Mutant Ninja Turtles (TMNT).

Then, there are the painful stories I hear with increasing frequency about children who experience real-world violence: a preschooler involved in a serious automobile accident caused by a speeding drunk driver; a five-year-old whose teenage sister committed suicide; a child who saw a dead homeless person on his way to day care one morning; a boy who saw his father stab his mother.

The changed environment in which young children are growing up affects the very foundation they build for understanding how people should treat each other. There is a growing awareness that more and more children are not developing the skills they need to live together in peace or to resolve their conflicts in nonviolent ways. And, now more than ever, they seem to need help in learning how to do so.

More and more conflict resolution training programs have been springing up around the country in response to increasing aggression and violence among children in their homes, schools, and communities. But most of the programs are for children in upper elementary grades through high school, not for children under eight years old. Perhaps this is because as children get older their failure to learn positive social skills causes more problems for adults and becomes potentially more dangerous to others. It may also be that, because of how older children think and learn, it often seems easier to teach them specific behavioral skills through direct instruction and discussion.

Yet children do not start learning about peace and conflict in the middle years. Even President Clinton and Attorney General Reno have argued that efforts to curb the rising tide of violence will fail if not begun during the first years of a child's life. The foundation for understanding how people should treat each other and deal with their conflicts is laid in the early years. It is on this foundation that programs for older children must build. Yet few adults have adequate, if any, preparation for dealing with the effects on children of increased violence in society, much less for teaching children how to live with others peacefully. Learning to do so is an enormous challenge for us all. Indeed, nothing can substitute for changing the factors in society that are bombarding young children with violence and undermining their development of positive social skills. And, when it comes to teaching concepts as complex and emotionally loaded as peace and violence, there are no easy answers. We have barely begun to learn what to do, and few resources exist to help with the process.

Rather than providing complete answers, then, I hope this book will contribute to the growing efforts and dialogue among concerned and committed adults around the country about how to break the cycle of violence in children's lives. It is not without ambivalence that I am writing it. I wish that, in the twenty-five years since I lost my innocence in the Detroit riots, the need for this book had dwindled rather than mushroomed.

ASSUMPTIONS THAT GUIDE THIS BOOK

This book aims to help you in your daily efforts to teach children to live peacefully in this violent world. It grows out of several basic assumptions about young children and how they can best learn about peace and conflict resolution in violent times:

Prevention and Intervention Go Hand in Hand Efforts to break the cycle of violence have to focus as much on *prevention*—i.e., teaching young children how to live peacefully—as on *intervention*—i.e., helping children make sense of and work through the violence in their lives. Daily, children are taught violent lessons about resolving conflicts from the world around them. To reduce the negative effects of that violence, we need to place lessons about peace and conflict resolution at the heart of our daily work. Toward this end, this book is organized around the idea of creating *Peaceable Classrooms** with young children. A Peaceable Classroom is a place where children learn how to live together in a respectful and empowering classroom community. It involves infusing trust and safety, responsibility, mutual respect, and cooperation into all aspects of the classroom.

The Roots of Global and Democratic Education Peaceable Classrooms provide the best possible foundation for helping children to become participating members of a democratic and global community. What young children learn about how to treat others becomes a cornerstone they will use for deciding how to treat others when they are adults. Similarly, learning how to deal effectively and nonviolently with the small, concrete problems they face in their immediate world will help them devel-op the conceptual framework they need to find peaceful solutions to the more abstract and bigger problems they will face in the wider community in the future.

---

*
The idea of a Peaceable Classroom has been used by others. For instance, see W.J. Kreidler, *Elementary Perspectives: Teaching Concepts of Peace and Conflict,* (Cambridge, MA: Educators for Social Responsibility, 1990).

A Developmental Perspective For Peaceable Classrooms to be effective, they need to take into account how young children think and learn, so I start from a *developmental perspective.* We cannot just pour the ideas we want children to learn into their heads. They need to actively construct their own ideas—social, emotional, and intellectual—from their direct experience. How they do this is affected by their current level of development and the ideas they have developed before. Children incorporate positive ideas about peace and conflict resolution into their thinking when they are given, first, meaningful content for building those ideas and, second, content that challenges and confuses the ideas they have learned about violence and aggression.

A Holistic Approach to the Curriculum The more teachers embed the values, goals, and skills of Peaceable Classrooms into the overall functioning and curriculum of their classrooms, the more effective and far-reaching their efforts will likely be. Thus, I call for a holistic approach to the curriculum—where basic skills, concepts, and subject areas (including conflict resolution) are not taught in isolation from one another and where work and play flow into one another.*

Parents as Partners To the extent possible, we need to work with parents as we create Peaceable Classrooms for their children. Parents are often unfairly blamed for the violence their children bring to our classrooms. Some parents are as much victims of violence as their children are. Many more, despite their best efforts, are unable to fully protect their children from the violence that permeates society. Therefore, many parents need our support and assistance themselves. And the more bridges we can build between home and school in our Peaceable Classrooms, the greater will be our impact in promoting peaceable living for children and their families.

A Framework for Informed Decision Making There are few pat formulas or foolproof curriculum activities for creating Peaceable Classrooms —every Peaceable Classroom will look different from one day to the next and from every other classroom. Still, there are many tools and skills that can help you build a Peaceable Classroom. You will need to adapt them to the unique children in your classroom and the content they bring through a dynamic, give-and-take process. Therefore, throughout this book, I try to provide information that will help you construct a framework for making informed decisions about your Peaceable Classroom.

---

*   For a more detailed discussion of a holistic, integrated approach to the curriculum see S. Bredekamp, ed., *Developmentally Appropriate Practice in Early Childhood Programs Serving Children from Birth through Age 8* (Expanded Edition) Washington, DC: (National Association for the Education of Young Children, 1987), and L. Katz and S. Chard, *Engaging Children's Minds: The Project Approach,* (Norwood, NJ: Ablex, 1989).

A Note of Realism Finally, I assume (actually, I know) that your efforts to create a Peaceable Classroom will not be easy. We cannot single-handedly solve all the problems that violence creates for young children or for parents, teachers, or administrators. Here are complex, difficult, often scary issues to take on. Your efforts will often be ground breaking and sometimes controversial. There will not always be obvious solutions to the problems that arise. You will be striving to create a classroom that looks very different from the ones you attended when you were in school, and for many of you, very different from the kind of classroom you were taught to create! In addition, you and the parents and children with whom you work will have very different levels of comfort, experience, and skill working together towards accomplishing the goals of Peaceable Classrooms.

So try not to change too much too soon. Start where you feel most confident and build from there. Expect failures and try to learn from them. See your efforts as part of the process of working towards a goal rather than being there. Team up with colleagues and other professionals with similar interests and concerns, so you can help and support each other's efforts.

HOW THE BOOK IS ORGANIZED

The book has two parts. Part I focuses on the key elements of Peaceable Classrooms, describes why each is important in itself and within the whole, and considers specific implications for practice. Part II provides a wide range of resources and practical ideas to help in your efforts to create a Peaceable Classroom.

Chapter 1, *Growing Up in a Violent World,* describes the violent world in which children are growing up and asks how this is affecting their ideas about how to treat others. What special problems does it create for young children *and* their teachers and parents? How can traditional approaches for dealing with conflict and violence in the classroom be modified or supplemented to help children learn skills for peaceful living in these times?

Chapter 2, *How Young Children Understand and Learn About Peace, Conflict, and Violence* looks at the developmental characteristics of young children's thinking about peace and violence. What are the range of ways they think about peace and conflict? How and why do these ideas develop? How do specific experiences connected with peace and violence affect a child's ideas and actions? How do children's ideas change with age and experience? What are the implications of these ideas for how we work with children on issues of peace and conflict?

Chapter 3, *Setting the Stage: The Peaceable Classroom,* proposes that to teach young children how to live peacefully, they need to experience directly what it means to live in a Peaceable Classroom community. What are the characteristics of such a classroom? Why are they so important to strive for in these times? What do they imply for how you and your children work together and for how you organize and run your classroom?

Chapter 4, *Give-and-Take: Building a Peaceable Classroom Through Dialogues,* describes how give-and-take dialogues between you and your children can serve as the foundation for building Peaceable Classroom communities. What do such dialogues with young children sound like, and how do they change as children get older? Why are they such a powerful vehicle for promoting peace? What kinds of topics are appropriate? How can you incorporate children's input into the discussions in a way that's compatible with your goals?

Chapter 5, *Peacefully Teaching Children to Resolve Conflicts,* examines the "win-win" approach to conflict resolution. How do the premises and goals of Peaceable Classrooms guide efforts to teach young children conflict resolution skills? How do young children understand their conflicts and the conflict resolution process? How can you teach them, in a manner appropriate to their current level of understanding, to resolve their conflicts peacefully?

Chapter 6, *Anti-Bias Education: Helping Children Understand and Appreciate Diversity,* explains why the way you deal with diversity among people in your Peaceable Classroom will have a big impact on the ideas children learn about peace and conflict. How do children develop ideas about similarities and differences among people? How do these ideas affect their beliefs about how people treat each other? Why do they sometimes think and act in stereotypical ways, and what can we do about it? What are the implications for fostering an appreciation of diversity in ways that are appropriate to the children's level of development?

Chapter 7, *Facilitating Play: Combating the Negative Influence of Media and Media-linked Toys,* explores how Peaceable Classrooms can help to counteract the negative effects of media and media-linked toys on young children's development, learning, and play. What are the possible negative effects? How do media and toys help socialize children into violence? How can you promote play that supports positive social, emotional, and intellectual development?

Each chapter in Part II of the book, Practical Ideas for Teaching Peace, offers ideas for building curriculum around a specific theme and shows how to adapt them to your setting and use them to build a wide range of activities that advance the goals and values of Peaceable Classrooms.

I want to conclude by stressing that it is not fair to place the burden of coping with violence in society on children, parents, or teachers. Creating a Peaceable Classroom is *not* the solution to that violence. But, in these times, creating a Peaceable Classroom can make an important contribution to peace and nonviolence in young children's lives now and in whom they become as they grow up. And not doing so seems like a far worse choice.

Chapter 1

GROWING UP IN A VIOLENT WORLD

The day after the war in the Persian Gulf began, four four-year-old boys are sitting around a table in their classroom. Without warning they jump up and run around the room, making threatening karate chop gestures and sounds at the other children. A teacher runs over to quell the disturbance. The boys call out simultaneously, "I'm Leonardo!" "I'm Donatello!" "I'm Michelangelo!" "I'm Raphael!" (These are the names of the Teenage Mutant Ninja Turtles.) "We're killing Saddam Hussein!"

A day-care teacher takes a few of his four-year-old children on a shopping trip to buy food for a cooking project. At the checkout counter one child runs up to the teacher, grabs his leg, and starts to cry. The teacher sees a police officer coming into the store. He knows that two nights earlier two police officers came to the child's home and arrested his father for armed robbery.

THE EPIDEMIC OF VIOLENCE IN CHILDREN'S LIVES*

According to testimony before the 1993 Joint Senate-House Hearing on Keeping Every Child Safe: Curbing the Epidemic of Violence, the United States is the most violent nation on earth. It leads the world in assaults and rapes, as well as homicides, with at least three killings every hour. That is equal to more than 25,000 homicides a year, or half the number of U.S. deaths in the whole Vietnam War.

---

* The facts and figures about violence listed here come from the following sources: C. Dodd and M.R. Edelman, testimony before the Joint Senate-House Hearing on Keeping Every Child Safe: Curbing the Epidemic of Violence, 103rd Congress, 1st session, 10 March 1993; J. Garbarino et al., *Children in Danger: Coping with the Effects of Community Violence,* (San Francisco: Jossey-Bass, 1992); Children's Defense Fund, *The State of America's Children,* (Washington, DC: Children's Defense Fund, 1992); B. Groves et al., "Silent Victims: Children Who Witness Violence," *Journal of the American Medical Association* 269, no. 2 (13 January 1993): 262-264; National Association for the Education of Young Children, "Position Statement on Violence in the Lives of Children," *Young Children* 48, no. 6 (September 1993): 80-84; T. Weiner, "Senate Unit Calls U.S. Most Violent Country," *Boston Globe,* 13 March 1991; and Zero to Three, *Can They Hope to Feel Safe Again? Impact of Violence on Infants, Toddlers, Their Parents, and Practitioners,* (Arlington, VA: National Center for Clinical Infant Programs, 1992).

The figures on children and violence are especially appalling. An estimated 100,000 children carry guns to school every day. One child is murdered every three hours. A child growing up in urban Chicago is fifteen times more likely to be murdered than a child in Northern Ireland. In 1991, 2.7 million children were reported to child protection agencies as victims of neglect, physical abuse, sexual abuse, or emotional maltreatment; nationwide the number of children reported abused or neglected has tripled since 1980. And this year over 3 million children will experience or witness parental abuse—ranging from hitting, punching, or slapping to attacks with guns or knives.

All too often this violence enters the lives of very young children. Research at Boston City Hospital found that one in ten children who attended the hospital's pediatric primary care clinic had witnessed a shooting or stabbing before the age of six—half in the home, half on the streets. And another recent study found that all of the children in a Chicago public housing project had witnessed a shooting by age five.

Whether or not children learn about violence from direct experience, they see an overwhelming amount in the news media. News stories show that people do horrendous things to each other, that they solve their problems with violence, and that world leaders and governments resolve international conflicts through violence.

The causes of violence in society are complex and deep. They are related to social and economic injustice, indifference, and neglect. Racism, poverty, substance abuse, the proliferation of handguns, and government policies that disenfranchise many Americans—especially children—all contribute to the cycle of increasing violence in children's lives. And, while efforts in the classroom to break that cycle can make a major difference in children's lives and the wider world, the injustice and neglect must also be addressed and rectified for deep and lasting change to occur.

DEREGULATION OF CHILDREN'S TELEVISION: MORE VIOLENCE IN CHILDREN'S MEDIA, TOYS, AND PLAY*

In addition to children's exposure to real violence, the unrelenting *entertainment and fantasy violence* in the media gives children large daily doses of pretend danger, war, and fighting that are depicted as glamorous, exciting, and fun. The quantity and realism of violence on children's television increased dramatically in 1984, when children's shows were deregulated by the Federal Communications Commission. Deregulation led to *program-length commercials*—cartoon programs developed to sell to children a whole line of highly realistic toys that replicated the characters and props on the show.

Cross marketing between videos and toys reached a new height when the popular and violent video game STREET FIGHTER II was marketed as a G.I. Joe toy.

---

* For a more complete discussion of many of the issues raised in this section see N. Carlsson-Paige and D. Levin, *Who's Calling the Shots?: How to Respond Effectively to Children's Fascination with War Play and War Toys,* (Philadelphia: New Society Publishers, 1990). The facts and figures about media violence and violent toys come from N. Carlsson-Paige and D. Levin, *Who's Calling the Shots?,* (Philadelphia: New Society Publishers, 1990); D. Scheff, *Game Over: How Nintendo Zapped an American Industry, Captured Your Dollars and Enslaved Your Children,* (New York: Random House, 1993); P. Tuchscherer, *TV Interactive Toys: The New High Tech Threat to Children,* (Bend, OR: Pinaroo Publishing, 1988); and the July 1990 issue of *Young Children.*

This approach to marketing toys to children has been highly successful. Within one year of deregulation, nine of the ten best-selling toys had TV shows. And the most successful shows were violent—one of the most popular, "Transformers," had eighty-three violent acts per hour. Others include "Masters of the Universe," "GI Joe," "Ghostbusters," and, most recently, "Teenage Mutant Ninja Turtles" and "X-Men." All of these shows have a similar underlying plot—bad guys attack good guys for reasons that are hard for young children to understand. The good guys can do whatever they want because they are good, and they always win; but they can never relax and feel safe because the bad guys always come back to attack again.

Young children have many opportunities to watch these violent shows. Between age three and six, they see an average of four hours of TV a day, more on weekends. By age eighteen, they will have watched TV for the equivalent of seven years, more time than they will spend in school. Children living in poverty and urban areas watch an average of 50 percent more.*

And when children are not watching violent TV shows they are often still involved with the violent images from the screen. The highly realistic toys linked to the shows channel children into replicating in their play the violence they have seen on the screen. And the marketing of non-toy products (like bed sheets, underwear, lunch boxes, and breakfast cereals) with the logos of the shows means that children can literally go to bed and wake up with their favorite violent media heroes, who keep the violent themes, behavior, and products forever on their minds.

The Teenage Mutant Ninja Turtles (TMNT) are the most successful example of this phenomenon of media/product cross-feeding. In the spring of 1990, when the first TMNT movie came out, more than one thousand Turtle toys and products were already licensed to be on store shelves. Receipts from these products were enormous as "Turtle mania" swept the mass culture of young children. The movie grossed more money during its first week than any other spring-release movie in history. The sales of children's meals at a popular fast-food chain more than doubled when it offered a TMNT cartoon video with the meal. And eight of the ten best-selling children's books in 1990 had TMNT titles.

In one study of how the TMNT affected children in early childhood classrooms, 91 percent of teachers who were surveyed reported violence and aggression associated with the Turtles.** They saw children being more

---

* These figures do not take into account the large amounts of time many children spend viewing videotapes (which are now in more than two-thirds of U.S. households) or playing home video games (there are now more than 35 million Nintendo systems in over one-third of U.S. homes). Both these media have much violent content, which is often tied into the violent TV cartoon shows mentioned above.

** N. Carlsson-Paige and D. Levin, "The Subversion of Healthy Development and Play," *Day Care and Early Education* 19, no. 2 (Winter 1991): 14-20.

aggressive in their play. And they said that both in and out of play children more often resorted to violence when conflicts arose.

Concerns about the effects of entertainment violence on children have led many organizations that focus on children's well-being to adopt strong position statements against media violence. These include the American Pediatric Association, the American Psychological Association, the Association for Childhood Education International, the National Association for the Education of Young Children, and the Parent-Teacher Association of America.

In addition, the U.S. Congress and the U.S. Surgeon General have been expressing growing concern about this violence.

THE CONTINUUM OF VIOLENCE AFFECTS ALL CHILDREN

Few children can escape exposure to the culture of violence that surrounds them, but children are exposed and affected to varying degrees. You can think of the violence in children's lives as falling along a continuum, as represented on the pyramid in Figure 1.

Some children, like the boys who brought together pretend and real violence by acting out the part of Teenage Mutant Ninja Turtles killing Saddam Hussein, may be imitating the kinds of violence they have learned most about—the violence depicted on news and cartoon programs (1 and 2 on the pyramid). Other children, like the boy who cringes in fear when he sees a police officer because the police arrested his father for armed robbery, experience violence more directly and often more chronically (3 and 4), but they are also likely to be exposed to the same media violence as the other boys (1 and 2).

The more frequent, varied, and extreme the violence children experience, the more likely their ideas and behavior will be affected by that violence,* and the more help they will need from adults in working through the harmful effects of that violence and in learning how to be nonviolent themselves.

A DILEMMA FOR CHILDREN (AND TEACHERS)

Given the context described above, it is disturbing that the lessons young children learn about peace and conflict from their environment provide the foundation for how they will think and behave later as members of the global community. The lessons society and popular culture are teaching to young children today stand in dramatic contrast to what most of the adults

---

* For a more detailed discussion about the cumulative effects of multiple risk factors in children's exposure to violence, see J. Garbarino et al., *Children in Danger: Coping with the Effects of Community Violence,* (San Francisco: Jossey-Bass, 1992).

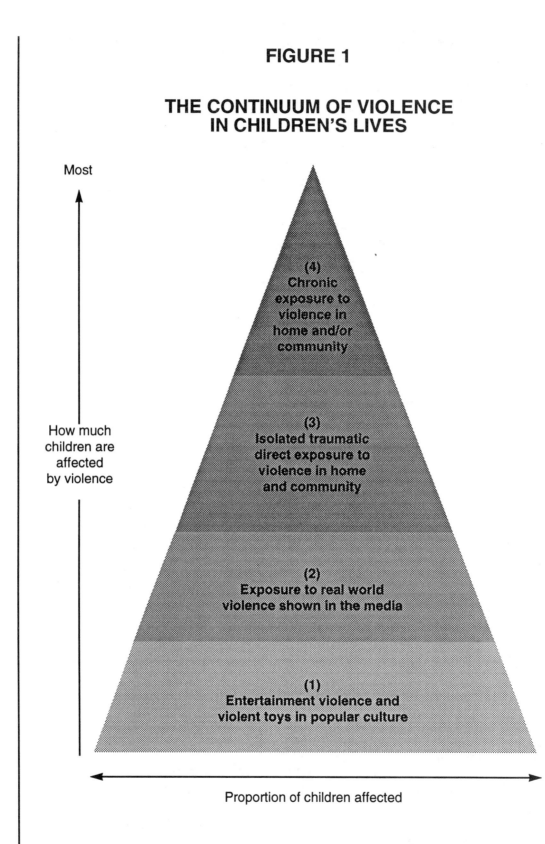

FIGURE 1

**THE CONTINUUM OF VIOLENCE
IN CHILDREN'S LIVES**

Most

How much
children are
affected
by violence

**(4)
Chronic
exposure to
violence in
home and/or
community**

**(3)
Isolated traumatic
direct exposure to
violence in home
and community**

**(2)
Exposure to real world
violence shown in the media**

**(1)
Entertainment violence and
violent toys in popular culture**

Proportion of children affected

in children's lives value and teach. It is hard not to ask ourselves, "Why does society seem to promote and glorify violence and aggression? Who benefits from perpetuating violence? How can a society tolerate it as a central force in the lives of its children?"

Figuring out how to behave presents a real dilemma for children. On the one hand, children daily get media messages that say: "When people have a conflict, violence is the best method for resolving it." "Fighting is normal, acceptable, and fun." "People are either all good or all bad." "Bad guys are bad because they look different." "If you are good, it's okay to do whatever violence you want." "In every conflict, there's always a winner (the good guy) and a loser (the bad guy)."

On the other hand, children regularly hear adults say: "Don't hit. You need to use your words." "It's not okay to hit to get that toy. You need to take turns." "That toy is for everyone to use. If you can't share it, you will have to use something else (or go to 'time out')." These dictates tell children to treat others respectfully and resolve their conflicts without violence.

But it is expecting a lot of children to ask them to choose our nonviolent approaches over the violent messages they are hearing all around them in the mass culture. As will be discussed in Chapter 3, young children do not have the cognitive skills to sort out these two divergent messages on their own. Our messages of nonviolence can seem quite impotent and dull next to the power, and often glamour, associated with the violence they see in the wider world.

To learn to be a responsible member of a caring and peaceful community, where everyone is treated with respect, children need many opportunities to build a repertoire of positive social behaviors, attitudes, and skills (see Chapter 2 for a discussion on how children construct that knowledge). As mass culture provides more and more models of violent and other antisocial behavior, and few positive alternatives to violence, young children are denied information that could help them build the repertoire of behavior and skills they need to behave nonviolently. And, as children spend more and more time watching television and using video games and less time playing creatively and nonviolently with toys and other children, they have fewer chances to try out and develop a range of positive ways to interact with others and be constructive members of a social community.

FINDING A NEW APPROACH

Today, many young children arrive in group settings with fewer skills for interacting constructively with each other than they had in the past. Often these children need a lot of help and intervention just to stay in control and not hurt themselves or others.

Yet, as will be discussed in greater depth in Chapter 5, many of the approaches commonly used in classrooms today to deal with behavior problems and aggression, like *"time out"* and telling children to *"use your words,"* no longer adequately address the needs created by the violence in many children's lives. These approaches often focus on restoring order to the classroom as quickly as possible so the "real" work can resume; they do not help children build the repertoire of alternative behaviors they will need to become more positive members of the classroom community now or the wider community later.

Carefully articulated and innovative approaches are needed to counteract the lessons children are learning about violence and also to fill the gap left by what they are *not* learning about peaceful living and nonviolence. A first step is to decide that *teaching social responsibility and nonviolent conflict resolution should be as valued and central a part of the early childhood curriculum* as the three R's and should be fully integrated with them. Only then can we develop strategies for teaching about peace and nonviolent conflict resolution in a way that will truly make a difference in children's lives today and, ultimately, in the wider society and beyond. Table 1 provides a framework for beginning to think about the lessons children need in these times.

TABLE 1

A DEVELOPMENT FRAMEWORK FOR PLANNING VIOLENCE PREVENTION FOR YOUNG CHILDREN

HOW CHILDREN ARE AFFECTED	WHAT CHILDREN NEED
Sense of trust and safety is undermined: *I am not safe.* *The world is a dangerous and scary place.* *I have to fight and be strong to keep myself safe.*	**An environment that feels safe:** *I am safe here.* *Adults will keep me safe here.* *I can learn how to keep myself safe.* *I must not do things to make others feel unsafe here, and others mustn't violate my sense of safety either.*
Sense of autonomy and empowerment are undermined: *Muscle and might, fighting, guns, and weapons are what you need to be autonomous.* *Fighting and weapons are what people use to affect the world.* *If I'm not strong enough, then I am helpless, and I had better be 'pretty' so I will be rescued.*	**An environment that teaches positive ways to be separate and powerful:** *There are many ways I can function as a capable and autonomous person.* *Here are all the ways I can have the effect I want without violence (or helplessness).* *There are many ways I can participate in decisions that affect my daily life.*
Sense of mutual respect and interdependence is undermined: *Violence is a normal and central part of human interactions.* *To need help or to help others is to be weak and vulnerable.* *We all need to look after and take care of ourselves.*	**An environment that teaches how to respect and rely on others:** *It is possible to be heard and respected by others and to hear and respect them.* *There are many mutually beneficial and cooperative ways people can interact and still be safe and competent.* *Here is what it feels like and here is what I do to live and work with others as part of a mutually caring community.*
Ability to understand experience and construct new skills is undermined: *I spend my play time imitating the violence I have seen, and my toys will help me do it.* *Entertainment violence [TV, Nintendo, videos] is an activity of choice when I have free time.* *There's no way I can figure out the violence I have I seen; it just happens.*	**An environment that promotes the active transformation of experience into personally meaningful ideas and skills:** *I can control my play and use it to experience power, control, mastery, and understanding.* *There are a whole range of satisfying and meaningful ways I can use my free time.* *There are ways I can work through the violence I have seen so I feel safe and in control.*

Chapter 2

HOW YOUNG CHILDREN UNDERSTAND AND LEARN ABOUT PEACE, CONFLICT, AND VIOLENCE*

Three-year-old Hari and four-year-old Jonah, usually inseparable, are fighting over a toy fire engine they both want to play with. After much tugging and pulling, Hari roughly grabs it and runs away. Jonah bursts into tears. When a teacher comes over, he screams, "Hari's not my friend. I hate him. I'm never going to play with him again!"

Five-year-old Kiki is on a walk with his mother when a very loud helicopter flies by. Kiki turns to his mother and asks excitedly, "Did that helicopter carry bombs?"

Four-year-old Jama walks past a homeless person who is holding a cup, asking for "spare change." She whispers to her father, "He's bad." On questioning, Jama explains, "Well, he's dirty. It's bad to be dirty."

The father of six-year-old Ralph is about to be released from jail to rejoin the family after a year. Ralph's teacher tries to find out how he is feeling about this because previously Ralph has said things like "Daddy's in jail, so he's bad." The teacher feels reassured when the discussion reveals that Ralph thinks people are bad when they are in jail and good when they are not.

During the Persian Gulf War a group of kindergartners are having a discussion with their teacher, who reassures them they are safe—the war is very "far away" from their city. Suddenly Jodie calls out anxiously, "What will happen to my grammy and

---

* For a more detailed discussion about how young children understand war and peace see N. Carlsson-Paige and D. Levin, "Children and the Crisis in the Persian Gulf," *Family Day Caring* (March/April 1991) and *Helping Young Children Understand Peace, War, and the Nuclear Threat*, (Washington DC: National Association for the Education of Young Children, 1985).

grampy?" It turns out Jodie's grandparents live in a distant U.S. city and can only be visited by plane because they live so "far away." Jodie is worried about their safety.

CHILDREN ACTIVELY CONSTRUCT MEANING FROM EXPERIENCE

Children build ideas through a slow process of construction. They do not just passively absorb information or ideas. As you can see from the examples above, they take content they see and hear in the world and actively transform it into something with unique meaning for them. And the meanings they make build on information and ideas they have constructed from *prior experiences*.

Kiki has seen a TV cartoon that shows helicopters carrying bombs, so when he sees a helicopter overhead, he actively connects the experience with TV to this actual encounter with a helicopter. Jama may have learned at home and school that she needs to keep clean, the way the familiar and safe people in her environment do. So when she sees a dirty homeless person, she immediately connects it to what she knows about clean and dirty. Her reaction could also be connected with a racial bias she has learned; "bad guys" are often depicted with dark skin in the media. The boys pretending to be Teenage Mutant Ninja Turtles trying to kill Saddam Hussein in Chapter 1 actively transform what they have heard about the Persian Gulf War into something they already understand, the pretend wars of the Teenage Mutant Ninja Turtles. The same kind of process is at work in the child who reacts with fear when he sees a police officer the day after the police came to his house to arrest his father.

EVERY CHILD'S IDEAS ARE UNIQUE

Because the meanings children make grow out of their experiences and no two children's experiences are exactly the same, *all children will make different meanings about their political and social worlds, even from the same experiences*. Ralph seems to have figured out a way to understand why his father was in jail and why it's okay for him to come home. But the fact that Ralph thinks people in jail are bad and people not in jail are good does not mean that all children at his age or level of development will think this way.

THE DEVELOPMENTAL CHARACTERISTICS OF YOUNG CHILDREN'S THINKING AFFECT THE MEANINGS THEY MAKE

While all young children's thoughts, feelings, and behaviors are unique, they are also highly influenced by the general characteristics of their age and level of development. As you can see from the anecdotes above, there are certain general characteristics of young children's thinking that make it look quite different from mature adult thought.

- **Young children tend to think about one thing at a time.** When they have a problem with others, they have trouble thinking about more than one aspect of the problem. For instance, when Hari and Jonah both really want the fire engine, that is the only thing they can think about; their long-term friendship becomes temporarily irrelevant. Similarly, when thinking about a particular idea, young children often focus on one aspect of that idea. Kiki thinks of one thing he knows about helicopters—they can carry bombs—not about another thing he also knows—that bombs and war are not a part of his life in his city.

- **Young children are egocentric.** They tend to interpret the world from their own point of view. When they see violence they will to tend to think about how they themselves, not others, will be affected. When they are in a conflict or feel unsafe, they usually will focus on—"What happened to *me*? How do *I* feel? What do *I* need to do to feel safe?" And because it is hard for young children to focus on more than one thing at a time, they often have difficulty taking points of view other than their own. When Hari ran away with the toy fire engine, he did not seem to consider how Jonah felt. And the Turtles who ran around threatening other children as they pretended to kill Saddam Hussein certainly seemed unaware of the effects of their actions on their victims.

- **Young children often think in rigid, dichotomous categories.** They see people and things as all or nothing—all good or all bad, all right or all wrong, all friend or all enemy. Something can rarely be more than one thing at the same time. For Jonah—who thinks you can be either friends or not-friends—Hari did something bad, so he is not a friend. For Jama, clean people are good, and dirty people are bad; therefore, a dirty homeless person is bad. And for Jodie, geographic locations are either near or far away from her; her grandparents are far away, so they are in danger if there is a war far away.

- **Young children usually focus on the concrete aspects of concepts and the visible aspects of experience, not the abstract meanings or internal, less visible features or motivations.** When they have a problem with each other, they focus on the concrete aspects of the problem, and their efforts to resolve it will usually be based more on concrete actions, materials, and physical features than on intangible thoughts, feelings, and motivations. The more salient and dramatic a concrete feature is, the more likely children will focus on it. Jama focuses on the visible dirtiness of the homeless person. His location in jail or at home determines whether Ralph's father is good or bad.

  Similarly, a concept like "war" can be easier for young children to understand than "peace" because of all the powerful and salient aspects of war they see. "Violent conflict resolution" (e.g., hitting someone) can be more meaningful to the young child than the more complex and abstract process of working conflicts out nonviolently. And when children see fighting on TV, they tend to focus on the weapons and blood and guts, not on the causes of the violence.

- **Young children often have a hard time seeing causal connections between two events.** This makes it hard for them to consider how their actions may affect others, especially in advance of performing the action. Similarly, once an event has occurred, it can be hard for young children to trace back to the behavior that led to that event. Jama does not consider why the homeless person might be dirty. Hari does not consider how grabbing the fire engine might affect Jonah.

- **Young children's thinking is static, not dynamic.** They have a *hard time performing transformations in their heads*—that is, they have trouble figuring out how to get from one condition to another. Thus, their thinking is more like a set of slides viewed one at a time than a movie where the movement among frames appears to be continuous. When Jonah says he hates Hari and will never play with him again, he is viewing but one slide—or one moment—of his friendship with Hari. Jonah cannot imagine that a transformation could occur so that Hari and he can once again achieve a state of "peace" and friendship.

CHILDREN'S IDEAS CHANGE AND GROW GRADUALLY

Children's thinking rarely changes dramatically. Rather, it goes through slow transitions from less to more mature thinking in each of the areas outlined above. *Change occurs as children have many opportunities to try out their ideas, see how they work, and then modify them based on what happened.* It also occurs as they have new experiences that give them new content to use in trying out and building new ideas. Table 2 summarizes the directions in which young children's thinking tends to progress.

TABLE 2
HOW CHILDREN'S THINKING PROGRESSES

From	To
Focusing on one thing at a time	Bringing in and coordinating many aspects of a situation
Egocentrism and taking their own point of view	Being able to consider more than one point of view
Thinking in rigid and dichotomous categories	Seeing that more than one attribute defines a category and that attributes can fit along a continuum
Focusing on the concrete and visible aspects of situations and ideas	Being able to imagine what cannot be seen and to think abstractly
Failing to make logical connections between causes and effects	Making logical causal connections between events
Static thinking—from one slide to the next	Dynamic thinking, where transformations occur as in the frames of a movie

Where children's thinking currently is will affect how you can best work with them to build their understanding of peace and conflict. Because children must make their own meanings, you cannot just expose them to more advanced thinking and expect them to adopt it. Still, there is a lot you can do to help children make new, more advanced meanings.

Implications for Practice:

☐ **The more your efforts to promote peace and nonviolence take account of the developmental characteristics of young children's thinking and learning, the more likely you will teach children meaningful and lasting lessons.** Try to start from where children are along the developmental continua.

☐ **The more your efforts connect to the unique meanings each child is making of his or her experience, the more likely you will be able to match what you do to the needs and abilities of the individual children in your class.** Try to start from the child's point of view and know as much as you can about experiences that have contributed to his or her unique meanings.

☐ **Efforts to teach about peace and conflict should point children toward what is to come.** Children's development and learning is fostered when their thinking is complicated—when they get input that challenges and adds to what they currently think enough that it is interesting but not so much that they cannot understand it.

☐ **Children need an environment where they feel safe to try out their own ideas, at their own level of understanding, to see how they work and need to be modified.**

☐ **Children learn best in a supportive environment that offers many opportunities to interact with one another and to build a wide repertoire of positive ways to interact.** When they interact positively, they feel the sense of power and connectedness so many of them sorely need.

☐ **Children need help getting content to use in constructing new ideas about their social and political worlds that counteracts the content provided by much of popular culture.**

FROM THEORY TO PRACTICE

The rest of this book focuses on how to use the ideas about young children's thinking described here to help the children in your classroom learn about peace, conflict, and violence. I know teachers are often told to use child development theory in their practice, and I know firsthand that this mandate is never as easy to carry out as it sounds. It is not an all or nothing task. There is always more to learn; and there are few formulae that can apply to all situations because each situation is unique, requiring new connections and solutions.

With a topic as complex and loaded as violence and conflict in the lives of children and their classrooms, it is vital to understand and use developmental principles if we are to forge meaningful and effective ways to teach children in violent times. Yet, learning to deal with children's needs around issues of violence and conflict poses a new challenge for many of us, so figuring out how to put theory into practice poses special challenges. In some cases, it may even require coming up with totally new ways of thinking about development and teaching.

At the same time, I have always felt a kind of purposefulness and power that few other aspects of my teaching can match when I have figured out how to translate developmental theory into practice. For theory has helped me to solve problems and make decisions about practice that connect deeply to children and meet their needs. It has given me a way to look honestly and openly at the effectiveness of my teaching. It has also given me a rationale for explaining and justifying to others what I actually do in my teaching. In sum, it has helped to keep my work with children and adults endlessly interesting and satisfying through all of these years. This has convinced me that it is well worth the effort here.

Chapter 3

SETTING THE STAGE: THE PEACEABLE CLASSROOM

Because young children learn by doing, learning about peace, nonviolence, and conflict resolution needs to grow out of experiencing directly how to live as responsible and contributing members of a peaceful community—a *Peaceable Classroom*. A Peaceable Classroom teaches children, through their own concrete actions and interactions with others and with the help of caring adults, what peace and nonviolent conflict resolution mean. It is a place where the teacher, while retaining charge of the classroom, shares power with children so that they learn from daily experience how to take responsibility for themselves and their classroom community. It is a place where teachers serve as a model for peacemaking for children. In such a classroom, children learn in ways that *match* their level of development, learning style, ideas, behaviors, and skills for living together cooperatively and nonviolently. Almost all aspects of the classroom can support this kind of learning.

No doubt, the principles and practices of Peaceable Classrooms described here will match things you already believe in and do in your classroom. But probably, some of them also will lead you to rethink current approaches and point you in new directions. Just as children construct knowledge and skills by building on what has come before, so teachers must construct their own vision of the Peaceable Classroom, both theoretically and practically. So as you read about new approaches that make sense to you, try gradually to build them on or change what you already do. This gradual approach will allow you to adapt and build onto the suggestions made here in ways that suit your particular situation, style, and group of children.

The group meeting described below illustrates key features of Peaceable Classrooms, and in particular how a teacher can work with children on shared decision making and problem solving.

A CLASS DISCUSSION ABOUT SAFETY

This discussion with kindergartners grew out of the unique issues and needs of one particular group of children. It took place at an end-of-the-day class meeting on a day three boys had had a fight over something that had become a stressful issue for the class. Before beginning the meeting, the teacher talked with these boys about her plan to discuss the issue at the class meeting, so that they could work out some agreement in advance about what they would like to happen. They were assured their names would not be used because of a class rule about not using the names of specific children at class meetings. The boys decided they felt safe talking about the problem with the whole class.

Teacher: I have been noticing something that doesn't feel safe. There are several children who make weapons when they go to the scrounge area. Then, when they're done, I've noticed that they start running around the room, pointing their weapons at other children and making shooting noises. That doesn't feel safe to me. When they do that, it makes me feel like the other children aren't safe. What do you all think about it?

Henry: I never do that. I always make cars.

T.: Yes, Henry. There are a lot of other things children can make at scrounge besides weapons. But I don't think we should talk about which children make what now. Remember, we all agreed before that it feels safer for everyone not to mention the names of specific children when we talk about problems? Right now, I want to hear how children feel when the guns are pointed at them.

William: I hit them when they do it. That stops 'em.

T.: It sounds like you don't feel safe when they point the gun at you. So then you want to hit them to try to keep yourself safe. How have other children felt when the guns were pointed at them?

Matilda: I ran away when they came after me.

T.: That's something else we sometimes do when we don't feel safe—try to get away. Anyone else?

Charlotte: I don't like it. Like, how would they like it if I yelled in their face?

T.: So you don't like the noises they make, either. How do they make you feel?

Charlotte: I'm scared and mad.

T.: So it sounds like children don't like having the guns pointed at them or the noise they make. And some of you have felt like you needed to fight back and hit or run away to feel safe. That sure doesn't feel safe to me. And you know our number one class rule: everyone needs to feel safe here. So we need to find something to do about the guns that helps everyone feel safe. When you have to hit back to feel safe, then someone else can get hurt. Then they're not safe. We've talked about that a lot before.

What are some ideas we came up with before about keeping safe that could help us now—some ways to make sure children aren't scared by weapons? I'll write your ideas down, so we can remember them all. Then we'll try to decide which ones we think we should try. [Teacher goes to a large newsprint pad on an easel.*]

Jules: Use your words.

T.: Okay. Any ideas about what words you could use?

James: Say, "Don't hit."

Melissa: I would say, "Go away. I don't like that."

Matilda: You could say, "I'll tell the teacher."

William: Say, "Go away or I'll hit you."

T.: You have come up with a lot of things to say using words. [She reads through the list for the children.] What other ideas do you have about what we could do besides using words?

Juanda: No guns at school. That's what we did at my Head Start.

T.: Yes, we could say no guns made in school. Any other ideas?

Manny: There could be no noises. I hate that.

Nick: Real guns are really, really, really loud!

T.: Yes, real guns make a terribly loud noise. No one can feel safe with a sound like that. And in here I've noticed the loud gun noises seem to stop the activities other kids are doing—that's kind of like their work time isn't safe. Any other ideas?

José: You could only make noises outside.

T.: That's another possibility.

Henry: You could only shoot your friends.

---

* The teacher recognizes that some of the children do not read, but the list still serves a useful purpose in legitimizing the ideas-sharing process, helping children focus on particular ideas, and providing an opportunity for the children to find meaning in the literacy process at their individual levels of understanding.

Tanaka: I don't want my friends to shoot me.

Larry: Only if the friend says it's okay.

T.: So you could ask your friends if it's okay to pretend to shoot them? [A few children nod in agreement.] Well, you all have come up with a really good list of things to try. It's taken a long time. So let's come back to this tomorrow. Let's come back to our list and decide which ones to try. You can even try using them during the day and report back at the end-of-day meeting tomorrow, so we can hear how they worked. And those of you who make pretend weapons and use them in here, see what you think about how the rules work for you, too. I'll leave our list up, so you can come look at it if you need to.

While this discussion took place in a kindergarten, the general approach could be adapted for both older and younger children because children will respond based on their current level of thinking.

WHAT IS AN EARLY CHILDHOOD PEACEABLE CLASSROOM?

PEACEABLE CLASSROOMS PROMOTE A SENSE OF TRUST AND SAFETY

At the heart of an early childhood Peaceable Classroom is helping every child feel deeply that *"I Am Safe Here"*: *my body is safe, my feelings are safe, my thoughts, ideas, and words are safe, and my work (the things I make and materials I use) is safe.* With a sense of safety comes a sense of trust, one of the most basic developmental needs of children, and an essential part of the foundation on which all social, emotional, and intellectual development builds. It has always been recognized as important in early childhood settings. *If children do not feel safe, efforts to teach them nonviolence will always be undermined.* And, in these times, when the continuum of violence that surrounds more and more young children is depriving them of the opportunities they need to develop a sense of safety, early childhood classrooms must try harder than ever.

The class meeting about safety and toy guns described above provides a poignant example of a teacher helping children learn by "doing" what it really means to feel safe. Before the meeting, she talks with the three boys whose behavior earlier in the day led to her decision to hold a meeting on this topic; this helps them feel safe during the meeting and shows them they can work on the issue together in a nonpunitive, blame-free manner. Early in the meeting, when Henry begins to focus on things that could lead to casting blame, she provides reassurance that names will not be used "so everyone feels safe." She often refers to safety in her efforts to further the children's thinking about the toy guns—whether the noises and gestures of others pointing guns feel safe, whether work time feels safe, why hitting others to deal with a problem cannot be allowed. She also conveys through all of her words her *deep care and respect* for every child, prerequisites for helping them learn to feel safe.

Implications for Practice:

☐ **Help young children make a smooth and secure transition from home to school; this is at the heart of learning to feel safe at school.*** Until they have established a sense of safety and trust, your other teaching efforts can be undermined.

- Try to build bridges between home and school with *familiar transition objects,* such as stuffed animals and family photos.

- Put out *play materials* that are likely to be part of their prior experiences—felt-tipped markers, play dough and toy animals, baby dolls and toy vehicles—and culturally relevant to their family backgrounds. Both Chapter 6 and Chapter 7 discuss culture and play more fully.

- Establish *rituals* that help children say "good-bye" to parents in the morning and "hello" at the end of the day—putting the child's picture up on the attendance board in the morning and taking it down when it is time to go home, a special good-bye wave to each other at a window.

- Have a *regular sequence of activities* during the day, so children quickly learn the rhythms of the day, and when to expect their caretakers to return at the end of the day. In Chapter 9, Figure 11, "Our Daily Schedule" provides an example of one way to help make children comfortable with the day's activities.

- *Talk to parents* or other primary caretakers in advance about what they think will help their particular child feel safe in school.

---

* For a comprehensive discussion of how to work on this issue in developmentally appropriate ways, see N. Balaban, *Starting School: From Separation to Independence,* (New York: Teachers College Press, 1985).

☐ **Help each child learn, as quickly as possible, to rely on you to ensure her or his safety.** Young children look to adults to keep them safe. They need to know you are there, especially when they feel directly threatened. When children see you as a supportive and respectful adult they feel secure, which frees them up to explore, experiment, and take risks. You also will provide a powerful model of how people in a peaceable community treat each other, which children can gradually learn to emulate.

☐ **Create concrete and meaningful rules, rituals, and routines that provide predictability, consistency, and order in the classroom.** This helps children feel secure because they know how both they and others are expected to behave. Like the teacher in the discussion about safety, to the extent possible involve children in creating and modifying the rules. See Chapter 4 for some suggestions for rules and routines to use in Peaceable Classrooms. There are additional ideas for how to establish rules and routines in Part II of this book.

☐ **Throughout the year, build bridges between the children's homes and the classroom.** The more you connect what you do in the classroom to what the children already know or care about from home, the more likely they will feel safe. Similarly, the more parents feel they understand and play a role in what happens in their child's classroom, the more likely they will feel the classroom is a safe place for their child.

☐ **Teach every child what it means to keep oneself and others safe; one powerful organizer for this is the "Safety Rule."** A major task of the Peaceable Classroom's curriculum is helping children learn how to keep themselves and others safe. As we saw in the earlier discussion, where the Safety Rule was used to distinguish appropriate from inappropriate behavior, it can help children learn in developmentally appropriate ways about how to live safely and peacefully in a community. The teacher leading the discussion had the Safety Rule—'we need to feel safe here'—at the top of the list of class rules. And especially at the beginning of the year, when she was creating the Peaceable Classroom with her children, she emphasized teaching the children how to put it into action.

- Teach children how to keep their own and others' bodies, ideas, feelings, work, and possessions safe.

- Help children learn to use the Safety Rule to decide on appropriate behavior for themselves and others. It also can help children actively construct knowledge about living peacefully without imposing adult thinking on them.

PEACEABLE CLASSROOMS HELP CHILDREN FUNCTION AS AUTONOMOUS AND CAPABLE INDIVIDUALS

Children gradually learn to take responsibility for their actions and feel confident enough to formulate and share their thoughts and feelings. You can increase their sense of autonomy and competence by structuring many opportunities for them to learn how to function as separate individuals, have a significant impact on what happens to their environment and themselves, and make a meaningful contribution to the overall life of their classrooms. Helping children feel autonomous and effectual often involves sharing with them in safe ways some of the power and control that has traditionally belonged to teachers. This does not mean giving up your role as leader; you still must maintain order, purpose, and safety in the classroom.

There are many ways you can promote a sense in children that they are important and contributing members of the classroom during class discussions like the one on safety. Constantly ask for their ideas. Acknowledge and validate each child's comment by reflecting it back to the group, writing it down on paper, considering aloud how it might work in practice, encouraging children to put their ideas into action the next day. When a comment is made that diverts the discussion or describes unacceptable behavior (e.g., hitting), respectfully acknowledge what the child says before trying to transform the idea into something more positive.

Implications for Practice:

☐ **Provide children with many opportunities to take responsibility, feel important, and make the classroom their own.** For instance, you can do the following:

- Ask for and use the children's input into decisions about the classroom, but be prepared to give up some of your power and not always do things exactly as you would do them on your own.

- Teach the children to help maintain the room and the materials in it. In Chapter 9, Figure 9, "Class Cleanup Jobs" and Figure 12, "Helper Chart" show two ways teachers have worked on this.

- Involve them in food and snack preparation—setting and clearing tables, cooking and serving food, and washing dishes.

- Both indoors and outside, use simple cooperative games that promote give-and-take actions and encourage children to work together for shared goals. Chapter 10 describes how to develop these kinds of "class games."

- Help them share with classmates their contributions and accomplishments in and out of the classroom—for instance, children can share at meetings, teach others a special skill, and put things they would like others to see on a "sharing shelf."

- Ask them their opinions and ideas when you can appropriately involve the children in making decisions about the class. Many of the give-and-take dialogues in this book illustrate teachers' efforts to do this.

PEACEABLE CLASSROOMS TEACH CHILDREN MUTUAL RESPECT AND INTERDEPENDENCE

A Peaceable Classroom is more than a group of autonomously functioning children who merely do not harm each other. It also is a group of children who develop a sense of connectedness and mutuality with others. Learning to respect others and contribute to their well-being is not an easy task for young children. They are egocentric and only gradually learn to decenter and take another point of view. And young children also have a hard time understanding how their actions affect others or imagining what they cannot actually see.

The class meeting on safety contains many examples of how Peaceable Classrooms promote children's sense of connectedness in ways that match how they think. At the beginning of the discussion, the teacher presents the toy weapons as a *problem shared* by the whole group. She constantly shows the children how their ideas and actions affect others by asking them to state exactly how they experience what others do—"When they do that [pointing cardboard guns] it makes me feel like other children aren't safe. What do you all think about it?" Later, she helps children see that solving the problem requires all of them, not just the children who created the problem, to try new things. She also tries to incorporate all the children's ideas into the solution—for instance, by writing their ideas down and referring back to them later. Finally, by the very nature of the give-and-take dialogue, where multiple points of view are expressed and respected, children have many opportunities to experience the *value of everyone's diverse contributions* to the well-being of the group.

Implications for Practice:

☐ **Help children learn to rely on each other, not just you or other adults, when they need assistance or have a problem.** Group meeting times, cleanup times, small group project times all provide opportunities for helping children learn to do this. (See "A Discussion of What You Need to Do When You Need Help" in Chapter 4, and Figure 12, Chapter 9.)

☐ **Plan developmentally appropriate activities that foster cooperation and interdependence.** For instance,

- Instead of having an easel for one child on each side, try creating one where two children can work side by side, sharing the same paints.

- Replace single-child swings with a tire swing that works best when three children use it together.

- Organize cleanup tasks so children need to work in pairs or threes. (See Figure 9, "Class Cleanup Chart" in Chapter 8 for one example of how and Chapter 10, *Class Games: Promoting Cooperation, Perspective Taking, and a Sense of Community*.)

PEACEABLE CLASSROOMS TEACH CHILDREN HOW TO LIVE AND PARTICIPATE IN A DEMOCRATIC COMMUNITY

Children's experience of how groups of people work together—for instance, distributing power and resources, making decisions, and solving problems—lays the foundation for how they will participate in groups and the wider society throughout their lives. Thus, Peaceable Classrooms create many developmentally appropriate opportunities for young children to build an understanding of the rules, rights, and responsibilities of living in a democracy. For example, through participating in shared decision making, children take the first steps towards understanding of the process of voting in a democracy.

Similarly, the group meeting created by the teacher in the "Class Discussion About Safety" models life in a democracy in the form children can best understand—concrete decision making in the here and now, with an issue the children really care about. Except for firmly limiting hitting (which endangers children's safety) the teacher does not impose her will on the children. She conveys genuine interest in the decisions they come up with and creates mechanisms for a continuous process—like writing their ideas down about "words to use" so they can be referred to later and making sure children know to expect another meeting to continue their work on the problem (and solution). In these ways, she shares power with children while maintaining her vital roles as leader and authority (but not authoritarian leader). And because the children will actually get to put their ideas into practice, they will have developmentally appropriate opportunities to test out and modify their ideas.

Implications for Practice:

☐ **Help children learn to participate in the ongoing process of developing rules and rituals and solving problems that come up in the classroom.**

- Use small and large group problem-solving discussions as a vehicle for working on meaningful issues together.

- Devise plans with the children for trying out their ideas and seeing how they work.

- Revisit the issue periodically to evaluate how the children's solutions are working and modify them as needed.

☐ **Involve children in problem solving only if you are genuinely interested in their solutions and intend to use them**. There will be issues you have a bottom line about or that, for whatever reason, you have already decided. For instance, children's physical safety is not negotiable. While such issues are rare, be honest with children when they come up.

☐ **To the extent possible, develop similar cooperative and democratic approaches for working with adults in the school and children's homes**. Not only will this support your efforts to create a Peaceable Classroom, it can provide a valuable example for children of what the things they are learning to do now will look like as they grow up.

PEACEABLE CLASSROOMS: NOW MORE THAN EVER

Increasingly, children experience violence and are left feeling unsafe and out of control. They need help now more than ever learning how to feel safe *without* being violent themselves. At the same time, most early childhood teachers are struggling to cope with the effects of violence on children's feelings, needs, behavior, and ability to learn. Rightfully, they often feel overwhelmed and ill-prepared for this role.

These realities place unfair and demoralizing burdens on children *and* adults. But we cannot just close our eyes and ignore the realities. If we do, we make children feel responsible for keeping themselves safe from danger, which properly is the responsibility of the adults who care for them. One way for adults to meet that responsibility is creating a Peaceable Classroom. As described throughout this book, Peaceable Classrooms can be an effective and deeply rewarding approach for beginning to break the cycle of violence in children's lives.

Chapter 4

BUILDING A PEACEABLE CLASSROOM THROUGH GIVE-AND-TAKE DIALOGUES

Creating a Peaceable Classroom is a dynamic process. What it looks like and how it works will depend on the unique constellation of needs, interests, abilities, and experiences of each teacher and group of children. In fact, there are probably as many ways to create effective Peaceable Classrooms for young children as there are classrooms, teachers, and groups of children.

However, central to any effort to create a Peaceable Classroom is teaching young children *how to work together to make and abide by decisions about how to act and treat each other* in the classroom. One highly effective way to do this is through give-and-take dialogues about issues that are meaningful to the children. Here are classroom examples to illustrate how dialogues can be used. Begin to think about how you can adapt them to your own needs and situations.

A DISCUSSION ABOUT WHETHER TO HAVE A REGULAR CLASS "SHARING TIME"

In the following example, a teacher helps kindergarten children work out whether they want a regular sharing time when children can bring up their ideas and experiences at class meetings and, if so, how they think it should be structured. This dialogue helps the children learn to participate in group decisions and to share responsibility with their teacher for how their classroom functions.

Text	Commentary
Teacher: What we want to figure out today is, "Are we going to have sharing?" Yesterday, someone asked: "Are we going to have sharing?" Some kids called out that they wanted it, and some kids groaned and said they didn't. So we need to figure out what we are going to do about it.	• The teacher involves children in decision making about how they want their room to work/what they want to happen. **[This promotes a sense of autonomy, community, and shared responsibility.]**
	• T. tells children at the outset what they will be working on. **[This is an effective way to begin group discussions.]**
	• T. chooses a topic that comes out of a real disagreement among the children. **[Young children learn best from direct experience.]**
Raise your hand if you would like to have sharing. [Fourteen hands go up.]	• T. creates a clear structure for children to use to express their positions. **[This exemplifies a structured but open format.]**
Raise your hands if you do not want sharing. [Nine hands go up.] Now, I'm going to ask if you don't care—some kids might not care. [Six hands.]	• T. accepts the fact that thirty children vote, even though there are only twenty-two children in the class. She does not impose her adult notion of one child, one vote. **[This supports children at their level of understanding.]**
So fourteen kids want sharing, nine kids don't want sharing and it doesn't matter for six kids. Now we'll hear some of the reasons why you raised your hands for what you chose. Let's hear from the kids who do want sharing first. Why do you want a sharing time?	• T. summarizes the vote but does not focus on who won or lost. She helps children hear each other's thinking about why they voted as they did. **[This models an approach to problem solving where all win; fosters logical causal thinking; helps children take other points of view; conveys that their ideas are important.]**

A DISCUSSION OF WHAT TO DO WHEN YOU NEED HELP

In this give-and-take dialogue, the teacher tries to show children new ways to function independently and cooperatively in the classroom.

Text	Commentary
Teacher: I need your help. I have a bit of a problem and you all know me pretty well, you know the classroom, and you know each other, so I thought maybe you could help me solve my problem. Would you be willing to do that?	• The teacher starts by telling everyone the issue to be discussed at the meeting. • T. admits her own need/problem; this humanizes her and her role in the classroom. • T. promotes the children's sense of commitment and responsibility as contributing and valuable community members.
Class: [enthusiastically] Yes!	• Children clearly relish this task.
T.: Here's the problem. I've been noticing sometimes in the afternoons I get really grouchy. I noticed this happens when there are a lot of kids asking me things at same time—calling out "Teacher, teacher"—and lots of kids waiting for me to do things to help them. It doesn't feel good to be grouchy. After you all go home, I think, "Oh, I was kind of grouchy to them. I don't feel good about that." I was wondering if you have some ideas to help me solve this problem.	• T. helps the children understand her point of view. • T. explains the problem in concrete, cause-and-effect terms. • T. does not judge children for needing help; rather, she treats it as a problem they can all solve together. • Using an *open-ended question*, T. channels the discussion into brainstorming possible solutions—getting different ideas and points of view. She is interested in the children's ideas and does not imply there is one right answer or that she knows the answer.

Jenna: You could let people take turns.

- A good start, but child gives no sense of what this might mean in practice.

T.: How would that work?

- T. accepts answer and asks a question to help child connect her idea to specific actions and behaviors.

Jenna: People take turns—first one, then the other.

- A definite elaboration, but as is often the case with young children, it does not really solve the problem at hand.

T.: So your idea is that children wait to take a turn—first, I help one child, then another, then another. Okay. Who else has an idea?

- T. *translates* Jenna's ideas to the rest of the class but does not evaluate them. **[This can be a hard shift in roles for teachers, but as you'll see, it can lead to exciting results.]**

- T. keeps discussion moving; indicates she values diversity of ideas, not just right answers.

Jackson: You could line up.

- As with Jenna, he's thinking more about what children could do than how it would help the teacher's grumpiness.

T.: So you could line up to wait for your turn.

- T. again translates for the whole group. **[Translating helps all the children stay involved and follow the logic of the discussion.]**

Carlos: Raise your hand.

- Another solution egocentrically focusing on what children do. Children often focus on variations of one kind of solution and need help going further.

T.: Raise your hand and wait for the teacher—instead of calling out my name. Okay.

- T. keeps the brainstorming going at a good pace.

- Instead of judging the proposed solutions, she helps the children hear each other's ideas.

Ray: Raise both hands.

- Another solution that is a variation on what came before it.

Rosa: I would go to another teacher.

- A possible breakthrough to a new kind of solution—i.e., Rosa might be proposing something that takes into account what can help the teacher, too.

Tosca: Ask a child.

- A transition in "kinds" of solutions has occurred. This one considers how both T. and children will be affected.

T.: So you don't always have to go to a teacher—sometimes you could help each other? Do you mean like how you asked Kerry to help you find the tape you wanted to hear in the tape recorder?

- T. highlights the special cooperative nature of this solution by providing details and a concrete example of how it could work. She does not say it's better than the other solutions.

Tosca: Yeah.

Sam: Oh, brother!

- He feels comfortable expressing his (distressed) reaction to this approach.

T.: Sam, it sounds like you don't like the idea of not going to a teacher when you need help.

- T. spells out the meaning of what Sam said in an accepting, non-defensive tone. This conveys it's okay for Sam to say what he thinks even if he disagrees (because he's not being hurtful of another's ideas).

Sam: You better go to someone who's good.

- Sam seems to understand the practical implications of the children-helping-children solution.

T.: Someone who's good? Can you say more about that?	• T. asks Sam to elaborate on his idea for others.
Sam: You know. You ask someone who can do it.	
T.: So you think you should try to think of who's good at the thing you need help with so you can ask him or her to help you? [Several kids nod in agreement.] Who has other ideas about what we can do?	• T. makes explicit Sam's meaning: Children differ in how well they do various things. • The group is clearly involved with the discussion. They do not seem threatened by the idea that not all children are equally accomplished at all things.
Kendra: Make a list.	• An egocentric way to answer; she does not give enough information for others to understand her idea.
T.: Can you tell us more, Kendra?	• T. uses probe question to help her de-center and elaborate on her response.
Kendra: Make a list of who's good.	• Tries to spell out how to make the children-helping-children solution work.
T.: I think I get it. Do you mean we could make a list of who is good at what, so children who need help could figure out who to ask for help—so you would know who could help you? [There are enthusiastic nods.]	• T. translates Kendra's idea, making it clearer. She accepts children's premise that different children are good at different things. • She helps children see in concrete terms how they could put this solution into practice.

I think a list like that could really help me not feel grumpy and help you all get help when you need it, too.

We've spent a long time talking about this now. You all have sat still for a really long time. You have come up with so many good ways to help me. You have really helped me. Thank you. For now, let's stop and have snack. Tomorrow, we'll work on our helpers' list.

- T assesses how this solution might affect her, again helping the children de-center, and see how the solution can meet her needs, as well as theirs.

- T. decides it's time to stop because the children appear restless. She acknowledges the children's accomplishments by focusing on their positive actions (not just using praise) and does not blame them for their restlessness. She does recognize that more work is needed to put the children's solution into practice; but, rather than leave things dangling, she tells them what will happen next and when.

For a sense of how the teacher followed up this discussion, please see Chapter 8, Figure 6 ,"Class Graph: Did Anyone Ask You for Help Today?" and Chapter 9, Figure 12, "Helper Chart."

These two class dialogues, the first on sharing time and the second on how to get help, as well as the one about safety in the previous chapter, illustrate how to involve young children in classroom decision making. While the content for each discussion grew out of the here-and-now needs of the classrooms, the process of joint decision making remains a constant focus. And in each, instead of viewing solving class problems or making decisions as intrusions on the regular educational program, the teacher treats them as unique opportunities to promote learning and growth about issues of peace and conflict.

Implications for Practice: Guidelines for Group Discussions

Several underlying principles used by the teachers in the above examples guide efforts at give-and-take dialogues with young children.

☐ **Try to select discussion topics related to children's direct experiences and growing out of issues that have come up in the classroom.** This can help children connect what they already know to the discussion topic and see its relevance to their behavior. It can also help assure that the issues discussed are appropriate to the diverse family backgrounds and experiences children bring to the classroom.

☐ **Use a structured but open discussion format.** This can help children develop their thinking about a particular issue, but it leaves room for each child to bring in his or her own unique understandings and issues.

☐ **Create an atmosphere where it feels safe to express diverse ideas.** Because children have unique experiences in and out of school, they vary a great deal in their ability to participate in a discussion. Some children will feel unsafe speaking up at first. Many have learned to look for the one right answer to a question or problem and have had little experience expressing their own ideas or respecting the divergent ideas of others. The children will also have many different ideas to contribute on any topic. In an atmosphere that feels safe, where varying degrees and forms of participation are respected, they are more likely to take risks and try out their ideas with others.

☐ **Help children put their ideas into words and share them with others through give-and-take dialogue.** In this way, adults can help create a sense of shared responsibility and model for children positive ways to work on issues. They can also promote problem-solving skills and a sense of independence and being in control, which is especially helpful for children who have a hard time participating in discussions.

☐ **Establish rules and expectations for discussions.** To have successful discussions, children need to learn how to participate in a group. This can be hard for young children at first and is often best accomplished by making "discussion rules" a topic for discussion early in the year. Including children in this process (to the extent their age allows) helps them better understand the rules, and it gives them a reason to feel committed to the group's solution.

☐ **Ask open-ended questions with many possible answers and respect the diverse ways children respond.** Open-ended questions allow children at a wide range of developmental levels to participate comfortably in a discussion. As children learn that their unique answers will be valued and respected, they will get better and better at saying what they really think and feel, rather than what they think adults want to hear. At the same time, they will often need help making their ideas understandable to others.

☐ **Ask questions and bring in new information or ideas that complicate children's thinking.** The content you bring to discussions can be a powerful source of learning and growth. For content to be meaningful to young children, they need to be able to connect it to what they already know. At the same time, to promote the construction of new knowledge, what they hear needs to challenge their current thinking by providing a slightly more advanced perspective.

☐ **Find ways to affirm and validate children for whom group time and collaborative decision making may not feel comfortable or safe.** There will be a wide variation in the skill and comfort levels children bring to group discussions because styles of parenting in the home, cultural styles of communicating, and attitudes about decision making and problem solving vary among families and cultural groups. Children who have a hard time participating still need to feel respected and valued as you help them learn how to enter into the discussion. You will also need to keep the diverse backgrounds of your children in mind as you select topics for discussion.

☐ **When possible, end discussions with a concrete plan of action everyone can agree to try.** This can help children develop a sense of *empowerment*—the belief that they can do things that make a difference in their lives. And it can also help them learn that *socially responsible solutions* are both possible and satisfying.

☐ **Return to important topics from time to time to see how previous decisions are working.** Putting decisions into action, seeing how they work, and then discussing and modifying them with the aid of others can help children build new ideas and skills onto what they already know and also improve their ability to engage in a give-and-take negotiation process.

HELPFUL HINTS FOR LEADING SMALL AND LARGE GROUP DISCUSSIONS

Watching (or reading about) successful group discussions can create the false impression that they are easy to lead; in fact, they are not. The first year I taught kindergarten, I found running class meetings one of the hardest and most frustrating parts of many school days. When children had something to say, it was so hard for them to wait their turn to talk. They often went off on tangents that distracted everyone from the topic at hand. They said things only they could understand. And, most upsetting to me as a new teacher, it took hard work and skill (and sometimes luck) to keep a whole class interested and involved when they could not all participate at the same time. Without such involvement, discipline problems, chaos, and a loss of the sense of safety often resulted. I found the following helped lead to a successful discussion:

Prepare in advance for the discussion:

- choose topics in advance and decide how you will introduce them to the children;

- identify the children's likely key issues and ways of understanding the topic;

- plan questions that will get children to express their diverse ideas and will stretch their thinking;

- identify a variety of possible outcomes, so you can guide the children toward them, but also be ready for ideas you never anticipated.

Expect to make constant decisions about such issues as:

- what question to ask next and how to ask it;

- how to balance the needs of individual children with the needs of the group;

- how far afield to let comments go before bringing things back to the main topic;

- how to pace the discussion to keep all the children interested and invested;

- when to let "wrong" answers and values you do not want to promote go uncorrected in the service of promoting give-and-take;

- how to incorporate new ideas and information that extend the children's thinking while acknowledging and accepting what they have to say;

- when to end the discussion and with what group conclusions.

Offer children a lot of help (especially at the beginning of the year):

- learning how to participate in give-and-take dialogues;

- feeling safe contributing their ideas;

- staying task-focused in their comments;

- filling in the words and information others need to fully understand what they are saying;

- applying the ideas they get from the discussions to their everyday actions and experiences.

When more than one adult is present in your setting, coordinate your various roles by planning:

- who will take the primary leadership role for the discussion;

- the roles that will best facilitate the discussion—for instance, one teacher makes charts from the children's ideas while the other teacher leads the discussion, or one teacher works one-on-one with a child who is having a bad day and would do better not participating in the group discussion;

- specific ways various adults can help children who have trouble participating in the discussion—for instance, sitting next to them or making eye contact or whispering ideas for possible contributions they could make.

ADAPTING GROUP DISCUSSIONS TO THE AGES, DEVELOPMENTAL LEVELS, AND PRIOR EXPERIENCE OF CHILDREN

Following are some suggestions for adapting your dialogues to the ages and developmental levels of your particular children.

Preschool Children

The younger the children in your class, the more you and other adults will need to:

- **Carry out discussions in smaller groups, pairs, or alone with the child.** Younger children are not developmentally ready to spend a lot of time in large groups, participating in dialogues that require a lot of listening to others when they need to be doing and talking themselves. Discussing an issue with a few children—for instance, where in the classroom to keep the scissors so they do not keep getting lost—and then briefly sharing the decision with the whole group at a more traditional circle time can keep preschool-aged children active and involved.

- **Choose simpler topics and rules, and shorter discussions that are closely connected to the children's concrete and current experience.** The topics should be relevant to the children's interests, concerns, and abilities. With younger children, who are mostly concerned about one thing at a time, something closely related to what they (and not others) are doing at the moment is often the most meaningful place to begin. Briefly working on an issue when it arises, in a way that has immediate and tangible impact, helps the children involved learn the tools and power of shared problem solving. A discussion working out exactly what two children need to do and say to share a toy, devising a list for who gets to take the guinea pig home each weekend, or deciding who among the children that played in the block area will put away which blocks at cleanup time can be very effective with young children.

- **Give them more help working through issues.** The younger the children, the more difficulty they will have putting their thoughts, experiences, and feelings into words. And even when they can use words, because of young children's egocentrism, others may have trouble understanding their meaning. It is also harder for younger children to make logical connections between two pieces of information, come up with a solution to a problem on their own if they have not yet experienced it directly, or think about how their ideas might affect others. Thus, you'll need to give younger children more assistance than you would give older children. For instance, you may need to translate what a child says so it has meaning for others or suggest two possible solutions to a problem from which the children can choose. You will also need to provide more help putting decisions into action after the discussion.

Primary School Children

Some older children have had few opportunities to discuss and work out ideas in groups. These children's responses may seem like those of younger children. But they will probably make more rapid and extensive progress learning to participate in discussions than younger children once they are introduced to the group discussion process. Soon, most will look more like their more experienced age-mates. But, at first they will need:

- extra help learning how to participate;

- many of the same kinds of help that are needed by younger children, as described above.

REACHING OUT BEYOND THE CLASSROOM

Discussion topics that grow out of children's direct experiences at home and in the classroom are usually the most relevant and appropriate ones for young children. As children get older, the world outside the home and classroom will play a greater and greater role in their lives. And even with young children, there will be times when what happens in the wider community will be meaningful, and even important, to discuss.

BUILDING PEACEABLE SCHOOL COMMUNITIES

Peaceable Schools go hand-and-hand with Peaceable Classrooms. In such schools, *teachers, administrators, and parents work together* to implement at the school level the principles of Peaceable Classrooms and to support and enhance teachers in their classroom efforts. *Topics will inevitably arise in classrooms on which the whole school community can and should work together.*

At the beginning of the school year, for example, one kindergarten teacher had a discussion with his children about their anxiety over going out on the school playground at lunchtime (a common problem for five-year-olds entering a large elementary school for the first time). This led to a series of actions devised by the teacher and children that promoted a sense of safety and social responsibility in the whole school community. For the first month of school, younger children got older children as "partners" for lunch recess; teachers assigned to lunch recess duty came to the kindergarten to meet the children before recess; and a special area on the playground was designated for kindergarten children only.

THE COMMUNITY OUTSIDE OF SCHOOL

As children hear about issues in the wider community, especially those that threaten their sense of safety and well-being, they will need help making sense of what they have heard and figuring out what they can do to make themselves feel safe and even how to help others feel safe. Such efforts open up an avenue where children can talk about and work out experiences that are confusing or disturbing. Discussions of such issues can also be used to help children learn to create *Peaceable Communities* and to assume a role of social responsibility in the world outside class and school. All young children are working on issues of power and exploring how to affect their environment. Many have rarely felt they are important or that they can make a difference, either at home or in the community. Learning how to act on and help solve social problems outside the classroom in developmentally appropriate ways is a vital step in becoming responsible and contributing community members. And it can provide an alternative to needing violence to have an impact on the world when one grows up.

TALKING ABOUT ISSUES OUTSIDE OF SCHOOL

One teacher began periodic discussions with her kindergartners by asking, "Has anyone heard anything in the news they would like to talk about?" Children then discussed what they had heard in a give-and-take dialogue guided by the teacher. (The boys in Chapter 2 who were pretending to be Teenage Mutant Ninja Turtles killing Saddam Hussein had heard about the Persian Gulf War and could have benefited from such a discussion.) Wherever appropriate, this teacher tried to end these discussions by asking children for their ideas about what they could do to help solve the problem or help the people involved; as a result, they often took such action as writing letters and cards or planning and holding small fund-raising events.*

When you let children choose discussion topics on the spot, it is hard to prepare yourself adequately for every issue that comes up. One teacher of

---

* For an example of a teacher leading just such a dialogue, see J.B. Danielson, "Controversial Issues and Young Children: Kindergartners Try to Understand Chernobyl," in S. Berman and P. LaFarge, eds., *Promising Practices in Teaching Social Responsibility*, (Albany, NY: State University of New York Press, 1993).

preschool children who experienced a lot of violence in their lives had an unexpected group discussion when Ken brought up his visit to his mother in the hospital after she had been shot. All the children knew about the shooting already, so the teacher decided on the spot that they needed a chance to react, ask questions, and hear that Ken's mother was out of danger. Ken centered his comments on the beeping of the machine at the hospital (the heart monitor) that "told me my mother is okay." He had found something concrete to reassure himself (and the other children) about his mother's safety and recovery.

Ken's comments tell us what will best help him deal with this distressing event—to know his mother is safe. When they have a safe place to talk, children who have experienced stress and violence often tell us what will help them . This can help you figure out what role to play with a child. Ken's teacher ended this discussion by asking the children if there was anything they could do for Ken and his mother, and the children enthusiastically decided to make her get well cards that Ken could bring her on his next visit. Ken was thrilled.

LIMITING GROUP DISCUSSIONS

At times you will need to stop discussion of a topic raised by a child because it is inappropriate to discuss with a large group; for instance, if Ken's class did not know about the shooting, the teacher might have rechanneled the discussion. One way to do this is to *acknowledge the issue* when it is brought up and:

- admit to the children that *you need to think about it* some more and promise to return to the topic later; and/or

- tell the children you need *to talk further with the child* who raised the issue after the meeting (make sure you do) and will bring it back to the group later.

Either of these approaches is preferable to what one teacher told me she decided to do—put an end to group sharing meetings because of the unpredictable and often gruesome content children brought in.

THE ROOTS OF SOCIAL RESPONSIBILITY

For many reasons, give-and-take discussions like those described here can be hard to incorporate into your classroom. Learning to lead them well is extremely challenging, and no matter how good you are, there are always places where you could do more. You are never in full control of the direction of a discussion. It takes work to help children learn how to participate fully. And it is hard to fit the discussion into already packed early childhood curricula.

Yet, when you have successful dialogues on topics that are personally meaningful to young children, you are helping them work through their experiences and ideas about peace, violence, and how people should treat each other. You are also helping them establish a foundation for living peacefully and responsibly on which they will build for the rest of their lives. Learning to deal nonviolently with small problems and affect their immediate world today will give them nonviolent ways to solve bigger problems in the wider world tomorrow.

Chapter 5

TEACHING CHILDREN TO RESOLVE CONFLICTS PEACEFULLY

Conflicts are disagreements or problems people have with one another that usually lead to negative reactions and feelings. A central part of the curriculum in Peaceable Classrooms is organized around teaching children how to work out peacefully a whole range of needs, problems, and conflicts in varying degrees of severity. Therefore, teaching children to work out their interpersonal conflicts nonviolently is an integral part of all the principles and guidelines described throughout this book.

A DISCUSSION WHEN TWO POINTS OF VIEW COLLIDE

Nathan and Delise are playing hospital in the dramatic play area of their child care center. Delise, the patient, is lying on the bed with bandages (torn strips of sheets) wrapped around her head, arms, and legs. She seems in terrible shape as the doctor, Nathan, stands over her with a stethoscope:

Nathan: [Putting the stethoscope down and picking up a play syringe] You're shot. Your heart's bleeding. You need this to get it to stop.

Delise: No, it's gonna hurt.

Nathan: Be still. You need it to save your heart. It's bleeding really, really bad.

Delise: [Sitting up and beginning to pull off the bandages] No! You stop that. I'm better.

Nathan: [Jumping up and down] Hey, wait! You're gonna die. You need this shot. [He tries to push her back down on the bed.]

Delise: [Pushing Nathan away] Stop that. I'm better. I'll be the doctor now.

Nathan: [Starting to poke her hard with the pretend "needle"] You have to get this.

Delise: [Reaches up, punches Nathan, and bursts into tears.]

Nathan: [Yelling] Teacher! Teacher! Delise hit me! She hit me!

[A teacher, as well as three or four classmates, comes running over from the other side of the room.]

Delise and Nathan's cooperative hospital play has rapidly deteriorated into a fight. What started as a shared, mutually satisfying experience, has become a conflict where they both feel the frustration and anger that results when two points of view collide. Not only does the conflict abruptly end their play, it also disturbs the classroom, taking the teacher and several children away from productive activities.

The kind of conflict described above is typical in early childhood classrooms and could have as easily occurred twenty years ago as today. However, many teachers report that they are now spending more time dealing with such conflicts, which seem more often to lead to physical aggression and hurt children than in the past. Many children seem at a loss to resolve their conflicts in any other way.

"DISCIPLINE" VERSUS CONFLICT RESOLUTION TRAINING

After helping the children calm down, an adult arriving on the scene might deal with this problem in one of several ways. He or she might:

- tell the children they cannot hit each other—they need to *"use words"* when they are upset;

- tell the children to *"take turns,"* so that each has a chance to be both the doctor and patient;

- put the children in *"time out,"* where they can calm down and *"think about"* what happened;

- suggest a solution such as "Nathan, you have been the doctor, now it's Delise's turn" or "I'll take the 'needle' away to help you both stop being upset about it";

- tell the children to pick another activity.

Any of these approaches would probably stop the conflict—at least for the moment—and quickly return the room to normal. But they present some major problems. They provide short-term solutions because *they impose an adult's ideas about a solution on the children rather than significantly involving the children in finding a solution of their own.* Thus, none of them would help Delise and Nathan actively construct an understanding of better ways to resolve their conflicts in the future. And, none of them gives the children the feeling of empowerment that comes from figuring out (with the help of a teacher) positive solutions to their conflicts.

Additionally, the first three solutions do not take into account the developmental levels and abilities of these children. For instance, using "time out" and telling them to "think about what happened" assumes they have the cognitive skills to recreate on their own the sequence of events leading to the conflict and the logical causality underlying their actions. This is a tall task for young children, especially preschoolers. And, asking them to "use their words" instead of fists assumes they have had opportunities to learn the appropriate words to use in various conflict situations.

In short, none of the solutions suggested above follows the principles and guidelines for Peaceable Classrooms used throughout this guide. A different approach is needed, one where adults help children learn how to think about their conflicts and what words to use to resolve their conflicts peacefully.

A DISCUSSION ON WORKING THROUGH CONFLICTS WITH CHILDREN

Here is how the teacher who intervened in Nathan and Delise's conflict helped them find a solution to their problem:

Text	Commentary
Teacher: [Getting on his knees and putting a firm arm around each child's shoulders]	• The teacher uses his body to try to calm the children and reassure them of their safety.
Delise and Nathan. You're both really upset.	• T. acknowledges their feelings *without* passing judgment.
What's the problem here?	• He brings the focus onto defining the *problem*.
Nathan: Delise hit me!	• Nathan and Delise focus on the concrete aspects of the problem (the actual physical actions) from their own egocentric points of view, not as part of a shared problem.
Delise: He gave me a needle—he hurt me.	
Nathan: I had to. I was the doctor!	

T.: Oh. You do have a problem. The doctor needs to give the patient a needle, but the patient doesn't want it—needles can hurt—and they can be scary, too.

- T. helps the children define the problem as a shared one—in concrete terms from their two points of view.

Delise: [Crying] I hate needles. They give you a lot in the hospital.

- This shows how Delise is bringing her experience into her play; knowing that can help others understand her point of view.

Nathan: I had to—to stop your bleeding heart.

- Nathan tries to explain his point of view. [He shows possible confusion between the real and unreal.]

T.: It sounds like you wanted to help Delise get better, Nathan, but needles upset Delise a lot. They feel very unsafe to her.

- T. acknowledges both children's legitimate desires. When a child believes his/her feelings/desires are acknowledged, the child is more willing to listen and try to understand the feelings/desires of the other person.

- T. also helps make logical causal connections between them. In this sense, T. acts as a transformer—someone who helps static-thinking children get from a cause to an effect.

Can you think of what you could do so you'll both feel safe and be happy. We need to figure something out so no one gets hurt.

- T. focuses children on coming up with a positive solution that feels okay to both of them.

Delise: I could be the doctor—not him.

- Delise shows a typical preschooler's egocentric focus on one thing at a time—that is, what she wants.

T.: So you could switch jobs—you be the doctor and Nathan the patient.

- T. serves as a *transformer* for the children—helping them see how Delise's solution would affect both their actions.

Nathan: I think I should use bandages.

- Nathan focuses on what he (not Delise) can do, but his response does adapt to Delise's needs.

T.: Tell me more. How would that work?

- T. tries to get him to elaborate his ideas and think about how they could translate into practice.

Nathan: Use bandages on her heart—no needles. I'll make her better that way. Catch the blood.

- Nathan shows he has taken a lot of relevant information into account in his plan.

T.: Uh-huh. You could find another way to make Delise's heart better—without a needle—so she wouldn't be scared of being hurt.

- T. tries to make sure both children see how Nathan's solution would work and how it takes Delise's worries into account.

What do you think of that idea, Delise? Would that feel safe and okay to do?

- T. tries to ensure *both* children can agree on this solution and will feel safe trying it.

Delise: Good. I had a lot of bandages when I was in the hospital. And Nathan puts them on good.

- She can connect the solution to her experience—both in the hospital and with Nathan. This helps her assess the plan *in advance* of trying it.

T.: Okay, it sounds like Delise wants to try that solution, too, Nathan. So let's try it. Make sure you let me know how it works.

- T. asks the children to talk to him later which will give them an opportunity to *evaluate* how their plan worked.

Now, let's make sure you have the bandages you'll need before I leave. Which one do you need to use first, Nathan?

[Later in the day at a class meeting, the teacher has Delise and Nathan talk about their problem and how they worked it out. He hoped to use this as a chance to extend all the children's thinking about conflict, but instead the children all wanted to talk about their experiences with "needles."]

- T. helps them begin to put their *plan into action*—preparing materials and figuring out what to do first.

- Conversations do not always go in the direction teachers plan. Based on the intensity of the children's interest in needles, T. decides to take the discussion in that direction.

- In keeping with the principles of a Peaceable Classroom, he respects the *direction* provided by the children, uses it to help them get new ideas for *extending and elaborating* their hospital play, and makes a note to himself to hold another conflict resolution discussion soon.

This teacher does much more than stop the children's conflict by treating it as a discipline or classroom management problem. Instead, by using the basic principles and practices that underlie a Peaceable Classroom, he helps Delise and Nathan actively build skills for resolving their conflicts peacefully.

- He *promotes a sense of safety and trust* by acknowledging both of their points of view as legitimate, by not casting blame, and by staying with the children until they find a solution that feels safe to both.

- He *helps the children feel responsible and capable* by encouraging them to express their ideas, involving them in the decision making, and showing them how their own egocentric ideas can work in their present situation.

- He *promotes mutual respect and interdependence* by helping them understand each other's point of view and how their actions and needs affect the other.

- He *helps both children develop skills for living and participating in a democratic community* by taking them through a process that teaches them the precursors to negotiating solutions to disagreements.

- Throughout, he *takes their developmental level and needs into account.* For instance, he helps the children understand each other's point of view and he fills in information and connections between ideas when their static thinking and lack of understanding of logical causality could stand in the way of a positive solution.

TEACHING YOUNG CHILDREN A "WIN-WIN" APPROACH TO CONFLICT RESOLUTION

This teacher is taking Delise and Nathan through a process of conflict resolution similar to that developed around the country for older children. In this process, often called the "getting to yes" approach, the children seek a solution acceptable to everyone. But as you can see, he has adapted this approach to the developmental level and needs of young children.*

Here is the four-step process the teacher used in helping Delise and Nathan resolve their conflict: 1) defining their problem, 2) finding a solution to which they both can agree, 3) helping them put their agreed-upon solution into practice, 4) reflecting back with them on how they feel it worked.

Defining the problem

The first step in working through a conflict is defining the problem or conflict as a *shared* one, where there are two competing points of view. Until the children can do this, they will not look for a shared solution.

The way Delise and Nathan talk about their problem illustrates how most young children tend to think. They have a hard time seeing that their competing desires caused the problem—that Nathan's way of helping Delise scared her. So, when the teacher comes over, they define the problem in terms of static, concrete actions ("She hit me." "He gave me a needle. He hurt me."), not the underlying, less visible reasons for those actions.

Without assessing blame, the teacher helps the children see their problem as a shared one. He uses the concrete and visible aspects of the children's behavior to do so. Working within the confines of their egocentrism, he shows them they both have legitimate but incompatible points of view.

---

* This approach was originally developed for dealing with adult conflicts. See R. Fisher and W. Ury, *Getting to Yes: Negotiating Agreement without Giving In*, (New York: Penguin, 1981). For a more detailed discussion of the developmental issues involved in adapting the "getting to yes" approach to young children, see N. Carlsson-Paige and D. Levin, "Making Peace in Violent Times: A Constructivist Approach to Conflict Resolution," *Young Children* 48, no. 1 (November 1992): 4-13.

Finding a solution

The next step in the process is devising a range of possible solutions to the problem and choosing one to try—one that takes into account both children's point of view, is agreeable to both, and restores a sense of safety. Such solutions are often called *"win-win"* solutions as opposed to *"win-lose"* solutions (where one child's position prevails) or *"lose-lose"* solutions (where both children end up losers). Many children have more experience with the last two types of solutions, and find them easier to use, especially because of the many solutions like these they see in the media.

Furthermore, coming up with *"win-win"* solutions is not easy for young children because of how they think. It requires such skills as taking both points of view into account, figuring out the logical causal connections between the problem and the solution, and thinking dynamically [imagining how to perform the transformation from one state of affairs (the problem) to another (the solution)].

Despite these potential limitations in young children's thinking, with the teacher's help, Delise and Nathan can come up with workable *"win-win"* solutions that are their own—either to change roles in the play or to change what the doctor does (use bandages instead of needles). The teacher helps them think through how their solutions would work but does not impose his own ideas about which is better. He makes sure both children agree that the solution they choose meets his criteria for *"win-win"* solutions—that both children want to try it and both feel safe with it.

Putting the *"win-win"* solution into practice

Once children decide on a solution, they need a chance to see how it works. But first, they need to come up with *a plan for putting it into action*, not an easy task for most young children. It involves figuring out what each needs to do to transform the situation from a problem or conflict into their agreed-upon solution. So often, I have seen young children devise good solutions like "We could take turns using that toy." But then they have a hard time figuring out what each of them has to do to actually take turns because they both assume they can go first.

As Delise and Nathan suggest solutions, the teacher helps them clarify what each plan might mean in action. Then, when they agree on one solution, they already have a good start for figuring out how to implement it. And when the teacher ends by focusing them on the bandages, he is actually guiding them through the transition from negotiation back to their play.

Reflecting on how the solution worked and building on it

Finally, children need a chance to evaluate their solutions after the solutions have been tried out—a time to reflect on how well their plan worked, how they feel about it, whether they would like to change anything about it or *try something new instead.* Then, it is usually important to share what they learned with others. Not only does this step help them consolidate and expand on what they have learned and feel good about their accomplishment, it also promotes the goals of a Peaceable Classroom.

Nathan and Delise's teacher provides just such an opportunity for all these things by making their conflict a discussion topic at a class meeting later in the day. This gives both children a chance to present their experience and tell how their solution worked. But the discussion and input from others that could have helped them expand on their solution gets cut off by the group's interest in "needles." The teacher's decision to go with the children's apparent need to discuss needles illustrates the kind of *flexibility and power-sharing* that are constantly required in balancing the needs, interests, and goals of all the participants in a Peaceable Classroom.

WHEN YOUR EFFORTS SEEM NOT TO WORK*

Often, the children with "behavior problems"—those who most need help with the conflict resolution and other skills taught in Peaceable Classrooms—are also the ones who have the hardest time learning and using those skills. These are often the children who have been most affected by violence. They will often demand the most help, take the most time, and need your best and most skillful thought and effort if they are to learn to participate in your Peaceable Classroom. They often have a harder time and take longer to feel a sense of trust and safety in your classroom and have fewer skills for interacting positively with materials or other children. It can be difficult to "hang in there" with these children. To the extent you can persevere, however, most of them will greatly benefit from your efforts.

Still, even our most persistent and skillful efforts to help some children learn to resolve their conflicts nonviolently cannot address all the problems that result from the violence and other stressors in their lives. For instance, children who are experiencing what many experts now call "post-traumatic stress disorder"** will need more intensive and far-reaching assistance than

---

* For a more detailed description of the specific needs in school of children who are direct victims of violence, see S. Craig, "The Educational Needs of Children Living with Violence," *Phi Delta Kappan* 74 , no. 1 (September 1992): 67-71 and L. Wallach, "Helping Young Children Cope with Violence," *Young Children* 48, no. 4 (May 1993): 4-11.

** For more information on post-traumatic stress disorder, see S. Eth and R. Pynoos, *Post-traumatic Stress Disorder in Children,* (Washington, DC: American Psychiatric Press, 1985) and J. Garbarino et al., *Children in Danger: Coping with the Effects of Community Violence,* (San Francisco: Jossey-Bass, 1992).

one or two teachers, working with a large group of children, can provide on their own. At the same time, while there are limits to what you can do for these children, to the extent that they can feel safe and learn the skills and concepts needed to function in a Peaceable Classroom, they, too, will greatly benefit. And tragically, because the resources outside of school for helping children and families cope with the violence and other stressors in their lives are so inadequate, your efforts will be the best hope for many children!

Implications for Practice:

☐ **When possible, spend the time needed to help children work through their conflicts using a** *"win-win"* **approach.** Try to resist thinking of this work as interfering with "teaching and learning."

☐ **Plan your tasks and functions in the classroom so that at times during each day you are performing a "floater" role—going from one independently functioning group of children to another to facilitate their interactions and activities.** At these times you can work in depth with children who are having conflicts.

☐ **Make sure children know they can rely on you to help them work through their conflicts nonviolently.**

☐ **Find supportive adults in your school with whom to share and reflect on your conflict resolution efforts.** For instance, you might form groups where members take turns bringing in examples of conflict resolution work for discussion, or observing and discussing how conflicts are dealt with in each other's classrooms.

☐ **Keep in mind that the children who most need your help working through their conflicts are the ones most likely to benefit from it in the long run.**

☐ **Remember that some children will need more help than others learning to resolve their conflicts, especially at first.**

☐ **Become familiar with the resources available in your school and community to which you can turn to get help for yourself and for the children whose needs cannot be fully met by a Peaceable Classroom.**

BOTH CHILDREN AND TEACHERS
ARE THE WINNERS

One thing I've noticed above all else about children using the *"win-win"* approach to solving conflicts: *most children seem to love doing it.* They do not always say what an adult would like or expects them to say. And it is extremely demanding to figure out on the spot what to do and say next to move the problem-solving process along. Nevertheless, watching children learn this process has always left me feeling it is well worth the effort. Most children soon become fully engaged in the process of working out their conflicts, fully committed to trying out their solutions, and totally enthusiastic about sharing what they learned with their classmates.

Often, the children who most need help resolving their conflicts nonviolently respond to the *"win-win"* approach the best. Perhaps, what we are teaching is more novel for these "discipline problems" than for children who have fewer problems with conflict and, therefore, more interesting to them. Or maybe they realize that the conflict resolution tools they are learning will help them feel better about themselves and empower them to interact with others in more positive, rather than the usual negative, ways. In either case, it gives these children the developmentally appropriate help they need to change their behavior.

Teaching conflict resolution to young children can also be rewarding for adults. In the long run, by using the time you currently spend "disciplining" children to help them learn the tools they need to resolve their conflicts peacefully, you will free up your time to do more meaningful and productive things. You will also feel the satisfaction that comes from seeing the positive effects of your own actions on children's development and behavior. And you will know you are teaching the children who are most in need how to live as responsible members of a peaceable community.

Chapter 6

ANTI-BIAS EDUCATION: HELPING CHILDREN UNDERSTAND AND APPRECIATE DIVERSITY*

A TEACHER HELPS FIVE-YEAR-OLDS EXPAND THEIR UNDERSTANDING OF SKIN COLOR

Four kindergartners are at the water table, giving the class baby dolls a bath. The dolls are racially diverse. The teacher notices that all four children are washing the white dolls. Kim announces she is "done" with her doll and begins to wash an African-American doll. Jinan says, "Yuk! She's dirty."

Children begin constructing ideas about similarities and differences among people very early in life. The ideas they build are determined both by what they see and hear about diversity in their immediate environment and by the meaning they can make from it at their current level of thinking. And as you can see, when children feel safe to express their ideas openly, they do not always say what we hope for or expect.

We have all heard a child make what seems like a negative or stereotyped comment about other people. And, despite the values and attitudes we promote in our classrooms, I'm sure many of you have been seriously tempted in such situations to move away quietly, pretending you did not hear. It is often very hard in such situations to know how to react and what to say. But in this case, doing nothing is doing something.

In the previous narrative, the teacher might have concluded that Jinan, the child who made the comment about the black

---

* For an expanded discussion of the issues raised in this chapter, see L. Derman-Sparks et al., *The Anti-bias Curriculum: Tools for Empowering Young Children*, (Washington, DC: National Association for the Education of Young Children, 1989); B. Mallory and R. New, *Diversity and Developmentally Appropriate Practice*, (New York: Teachers College Press, 1994); and J.B. McCracken, *Valuing Diversity: The Primary Years*, (Washington, DC: National Association for the Education of Young Children, 1993).

doll, was racist—perhaps even that this is what she was taught at home (the "blaming the parent" approach). In such a case, she might have told the children to play with all the dolls because they all needed baths that day (the "color blind" approach)—thereby promoting the idea that all the dolls are equal and should be treated equally. She might have told them that the black doll was not dirty and given them factual information about skin color (the "teach children facts" approach). These responses attempt to deal directly with Jinan's apparently racist comment by pouring adult information about race and racism into the children's minds without helping them construct nonracist ideas through give-and-take dialogue.

Instead, the teacher went over to the water table and started washing an African-American doll herself and said to no one in particular, "I wonder what will happen if I scrub her really hard." The girls began to watch with apparent curiosity, commented that nothing changed, and then decided to try washing the dolls of color themselves to see if they could make anything happen if they "scrubbed *really* hard." When the teacher checked back a few minutes later, the girls reported in unison that they, too, could not get the dolls to change. In this way, she played the vital role of *helping the children collect and use information about the dolls' skin color that challenged their idea that brown skin is dirty.*

Because this was not the first time issues of race had come up in this teacher's classroom recently, she decided it was also important for the whole class to talk about "skin color" together.* So she looked for an appropriate way to work the topic into a regular class meeting. Here is the teacher's account of what happened:

> That day at class meeting, the children were taking turns telling stories about their "family pictures" (family photographs each child had brought in from home). One child commented that her mother was white and her father was black, and that's why she was brown. All the children began to look at their skin and the skin of their friends.
>
> A child sitting near a friend called out with great excitement, "We have the same color, so we're best friends."
>
> I asked him if he thought they were best friends because they were the same color or because they shared similar interests. He said he thought it was because they were both white.
>
> I wondered aloud if you could like someone who had a different skin color. Immediately, one of the children said with great authority, "Of course. Otherwise, my mom couldn't like me because she's white and I'm tan."

---

* Remember to keep the "safety rule" in mind when deciding how to respond to children's stereotyped comments. If what is said threatens the sense of safety of another child, it is vital that you deal with this directly in the here and now using the safety rule to guide you.

Another child jumped in: "I think you like to play with the one that's your color. I play with the white baby (in the dramatic play area)."

When I asked them to explain more, someone said, "You like your color best, so that's who you play with."

A white girl explained that "if you're having a baby, you usually have one the color that you're like."

And a biracial child jumped in to say everyone should play with all the colors of baby dolls, pointing out that sometimes baby brothers and sisters look different from each other and parents still love them.

The children expressed their ideas and concerns for a long time. "What if a lady with white skin wanted to throw her baby away because it had a different color skin? I wouldn't throw my baby away."

"You can't have a black baby if you're white, but there's something called mixed, and it could be mixed."

"Well I change in the summer so then I'm mixed too."

"I think you are what you are, and that's it."

I have been teaching for a long time and think I'm really good at talking with kids about hard and complicated issues. But this was one of the hardest discussions I've ever had. I never knew what I would have to deal with next. I always had to make sure on the spot, after each comment, if everyone felt safe. You know, the most important thing to me about my teaching is that the classroom is a safe and trusting place for children. I would probably never have a discussion like this early in the school year (it occurred in April).

But at this point in the year, a sense of community is really building among us all. An important part of that community is the children feeling safe asking questions, making observations, and talking about hard issues. The kids said things that are, or at least seem, racist. A discussion like that risks undermining safety and trust.

This teacher is describing how she used a give-and-take dialogue to help children express their thinking and build new ideas about skin color. Throughout, she facilitated the discussion by:

- maintaining a climate of *safety and respect*, where children feel comfortable asking questions and honestly expressing their ideas and concerns;

- *listening to and accepting* what the children say, even when what they say seems, from an adult's point of view, to be expressing stereotypes;

- helping the children *use their prior experiences* to discuss and clarify their thinking about this issue;

- trying *not to characterize* answers as *"right"* or *"wrong"* or merely tell children the "right" way to think about skin color;

- *challenging and complicating* the children's thinking about skin color without directly bringing in her own adult thinking on the subject;

- using the discussion as *part of an ongoing process* of gradually constructing an understanding and appreciation of skin color and race.

A LETTER TO PARENTS ABOUT A SPECIAL NEEDS CURRICULUM

Here is a letter the same teacher sent to the parents of the children in her classroom later in the year. In order to build bridges between the home and school, she often wrote to parents about what was happening in school. This letter describes the special needs curriculum. It illustrates teaching about diversity using the same underlying principles and practices she used in the above example. In addition, here the teacher is showing parents how their children are learning about differences among people, as well as how she is teaching more traditional skills, like reading, writing, and science, as she builds curriculum activities around the needs, interests, and understandings of the children.

April 23, 199__

Dear Kindergarten Parents,

The classroom continues to be a busy place. It's really exciting to watch the group at this point in the year. The children are so comfortable with each other, with the routines, with the expectations, and with themselves. It seemed like a good time to expand our horizons.

So a few weeks back, we began to look at people with physical differences. The kids seemed enthralled by the biography of Louis Braille and became very interested in Braille writing. We began to experiment, using a stylus to "write" in Braille. Then, we read Mine for a Year, *a book about a child who takes care of a puppy that is going to be trained to be a guide dog.*

This experience came alive when Hernandez and his dad invited a blind neighbor to visit our classroom. Pete and his guide dog, Victor, spent an afternoon choice time with us. The kids had prepared questions for Pete ahead of time, and he had prepared a little presentation for the kids, too.

I wish you could have seen the interactions between the kids and Pete. Their questions reflected a variety of issues. Some had come up from our reading. Others seemed to reflect the kids' feelings and curiosities ("What does it feel like to be blind?" "Have you been blind all your life?" "How did you get blind?" "Can't the doctor fix your eyes?" "How do you think about colors?"). Pete was truly wonderful. He answered their questions openly and honestly. I think each child was impressed by how similar Pete's life was to their own. He totally wowed them with all of his special "gadgets," such as his talking watch and talking calculator.

After our discussion, he stayed for the remainder of choice time. I'm left with the memory of Pete reading Stone Soup *(Braille adapted) aloud, with Victor and a few children stretched out at his feet and the classroom slowly growing quiet as more and more kids drifted into the meeting area to listen to this familiar story read by a new friend in a new way.*

Pete and Victor's visit was a special time for all of us. This week, we have sent them two class thank-you "notes," one that we recorded on an audiotape and one that is a Braille version of the same message—a new kind of writing lesson!

One extension of our work on blindness and deafness in the upcoming weeks will be to talk about how your eyes and ears work. We are planning a visit by a physician to help us understand these parts of our body. You'll hear more about that later.

WHAT ANTI-BIAS EDUCATION IS

These examples of building curricula around skin color and special needs show anti-bias education in action in a Peaceable Classroom. Anti-bias education:

- helps children gradually construct a stereotype- and bias-free understanding of people's similarities and differences;

- incorporates *all aspects of diversity*—from gender, race, economic class, and ethnic background to physical, intellectual, and emotional characteristics to thoughts and feelings and personal likes and dislikes—and includes what is sometimes termed *multicultural education,* but goes beyond it;

- informs all the interactions in Peaceable Classrooms because what children learn about how to treat others is highly influenced by how they deal with diversity among people and how they understand themselves as fitting into a global context;

- is *essential if children are to feel truly safe or fully valued* in a classroom, for if the whole range of appearances, experiences, thoughts, and feelings of one child are not respected, then any child can also feel vulnerable because of who she or he is;

- teaches children, at a developmentally appropriate level, *how to take concrete social action* that promotes greater social equality and justice;*

- constitutes what should be happening in the early childhood curriculum for the subject traditionally called *social studies*–but is infused into daily classroom life, not taught at an isolated time or as a prescribed set of facts.

WHAT ANTI-BIAS EDUCATION IS NOT

Thinking about what anti-bias education is *not* can help to clarify further what it is. It is *not:*

- pretending to be "color-blind" or to treat all children as if they were exactly alike and ignoring who they are as individuals, in all their uniqueness and diversity;

- preaching adult ideas to children about how to think about similarities and differences among people, because children need to build ideas actively from their own experience;

- teaching children only about cultures other than their own (as multicultural education is often practiced).

---

* L. Derman-Sparks et al., *The Anti-Bias Curriculum*, (Washington, DC: National Association for the Education of Young Children, 1989) discuss the importance of this issue for children and provide examples of how teachers have actually empowered children to take action.

ANTI-BIAS EDUCATION POSES
SPECIAL CHALLENGES FOR TEACHERS

While anti-bias education is at the heart of effective teaching about peace and conflict, it still presents one of the most difficult challenges Peaceable Classroom teachers face. This is for a number of reasons:

- Because many of us rarely talk about these issues ourselves, we have *few direct experiences* to guide us in our work with children.

- Anti-bias education carries the constant risk of children *raising uncomfortable issues* (e.g., liking people best who are the same skin color as oneself).

- The discussion can go in *unpredictable directions* (e.g., children bringing up skin color in a discussion of family photos, when there are so many other things to discuss about the photos).

- And, because *young children think so differently from adults about diversity*, when they feel safe enough to say what they really think (not what they think adults want to hear), what they say is not always what we are comfortable hearing. They will often *talk about similarities and differences in what seem like stereotypes to adults.* But sometimes the most outrageous statement can really be a question—an effort to get guidance, information, and a thoughtful response or answer from trusted adults.

HOW YOUNG CHILDREN THINK ABOUT
SIMILARITIES AND DIFFERENCES

As with all aspects of the curriculum in Peaceable Classrooms, the way young children think plays a crucial role in how we can best help them develop an understanding and respect for diversity. The same characteristics of thinking that affect how young children understand other concepts of peace, violence, and conflict (as discussed in Chapter 2), also affect how their ideas about similarities and differences develop.

- **Children begin to construct ideas about similarities and differences when they are very young.** Almost from birth, children learn by noticing differences. *They use similarities and differences among people, objects, and events to help them define and understand their world*—learning, for example, to differentiate a parent from a stranger, a bottle from a breast, or a rattle from a pacifier. They learn a label for their gender at around two years old, after which they start building an understanding of what it means to be a boy or girl—like me or not like me. By three they have begun to develop ideas about race and special needs.

- **Young children tend to focus on one thing at a time—usually, in this case, the most salient and visible aspects of similarities and differences among people.** This means that children will most likely focus on skin color to determine race and hair length or clothing (rather than genitals) to determine gender. With special needs, visible and concrete aspects of a disability (a blind person using a guide dog, for instance) will be more relevant and interesting to the child than less visible ones, such as the physiological reasons why the person cannot see.

- **Young children tend to think in dichotomies.** Someone is either one thing or the other (but not both) and thus either "like me" or "not like me." Subtle variations and shades of gray are harder for them to understand. *This can lead to thinking in stereotypes.* In the incident described above, the children struggle with differences in skin color that do not fit into simple dichotomous categories—a child who has neither his mother's nor his father's skin color.

- **Young children generally think egocentrically and concretely—relating what they see and hear about similarities and differences to themselves and their own experience.** The children discussing skin color above constantly refer to their experience with skin color as a basis for drawing conclusions about race.

- **Static thinking can make it hard for young children to understand logical causal relationships or the permanence of physical characteristics.** It will be several more years before they realize these characteristics are unchangeable. This can lead to misunderstandings about similarities and differences—for instance, that washing will change skin color or growing longer hair can change a boy into a girl. It can also lead children to make illogical causal connections—for instance, that skin color determines friendships.

- **Children's ideas about diversity and how they learn to respond to it are influenced by what they see and hear in the world around them about similarities and differences.** Because society—for instance through entertainment media—provides them with much very stereotyped content to use in constructing their ideas about such differences as race and gender, you can have a hard time sorting out which of children's ideas result from how they think and which result from what they have heard and seen.

- - - - - - - - - - (CLIP AND COLLECT) - - - -

PORTRAIT OF APRIL,™ The Ravishing Reporter
The Gutsy News Gal!
VITAL BABETISTICS:

Accessories: Ninja File Sai, Lipstick Nunchaku,
              Compact Ninja Star, Katana Blade Curling Iron.
              Kowabunga Camera, Make-up Brush Battle Bo
Favorite Headline: Beauty Queen Chokes on Crown
Weight: 99.9 lbs. wearing chains

      Flash! This just in: April is the world's most ravishing reporter. What does that mean? That means you're dealing with the gutsiest glamour gal to ever say, "We'll be back after these messages." April's one cool chick. She's got the power of the bob 'n wave – thanks to her real rooted hair. And what she lacks in brawn, she makes up in brains. This smart sister is super chic and turns heads wherever she goes. She never has a bad hair day when she's armed with her katana blade curling iron. It's bad news though, if this ravishing reporter hears a whistle in the wind from a flirtatious Foot fiend. She's got a detachable skirt that lets her kick low and high. And no kiss is as deadly as when April aims her lipstick nunchaku at a Foot face. Why would a bodacious bylinin' babe like this be interested in a Mutant Turtle? Well, as one source reported. "Cuz they're just so cute!"

- - - - - - - - - - - (CLIP AND COLLECT) - - - - - - -

CHIEF LEO™
The Flame-shootin' Feather-topped
Foot Fighter!
VITAL TEEPEETISTICS:

Accessories: Bodacious Bow & Arrow, Sewer Spear, Quasi Quiver, Totally Turtle Tomahawk, Battle Blade
Favorite Target: Shredder's Backside
Favorite Dance: Rain 'n Pain
Furthest Distance Arrow Shot: 112859 Meters (without a bow, too!)

      Those smoke signals mean war when Chief Leo hits the wild frontier. He's not a Cherokee or Apache; this Mutant maverick is in a tribe all by himself - the Turtle Tribe! And Chief Leo's got all the Indian instruments to make him a traditional wild west warrior. Don't sneeze at his feathery ceremonial headdress or he'll skewer you with his sewer spear. Watch the paleface Foot run for cover when Chief Leo pulls his fiery arrows from his quasi quiver. Then when it's trophy takin' time, Chief Leo uses his trusty totally Turtle tomahawk to give those forked tongued Foot fiends a close shave - very close. So fork over the wampum, dudes. Chief Leo's worth his weight in horses and tree bark pizza.

As exemplified by these two Teenage Mutant Ninja Turtle toys, the popular culture bombards children with rigid, destructive stereotypes about gender, race, and other diversity issues. Such practices only serve to promote stereotyped thinking in young children, thereby making anti-bias education more important now than ever.

Implications for Practice:

☐ **Focus both on similarities (what brings people together and what they share) and differences.** For instance, eating meals with a variety of different implements (i.e., forks, spoons, chopsticks, fingers) can help children learn that all people eat but in many different ways.

☐ **Start with a focus on the concrete aspects of similarities and differences—what children can see.** The "Class Graphs" in Chapter 8 show some ways to do this.

☐ **Focus on similarities and differences that are *connected to the children's experiences*.** For instance, young children discussing gender issues will be more interested in talking about toys girls and boys use than reproduction.

☐ **Try to utilize whatever diversity the children and adults in your setting provide.** Even groups that at first glance appear quite homogeneous can offer children many opportunities to experience a wide range of diversity. Food preferences, hair color and length, family size, and favorite stuffed animals all provide a meaningful basis for teaching young children about similarities and differences.

☐ **If your classroom lacks racial, ethnic, or economic diversity make sure to find meaningful ways to help expand children's experience in these areas.** Books, photographs, music, art, cooking, dolls, posters, class visitors, and field trips are just a few ways you can begin.

☐ **Provide children many opportunities to experience directly the value diversity can have in their daily lives.** This can help transform their common and natural tendency to treat differences with suspicion and intolerance. The "Class Graphs" described in Chapter 8 provide a highly engaging and developmentally appropriate way to begin.

☐ **Because children learn by noticing differences, rather than treating their focus on diversity as something to be avoided, try to use it as a tool to help engage them in a wide range of activities.** The narratives at the beginning of this chapter provide highly successful examples of this.

☐ **Challenge children's stereotypes, including those stereotypes they learn from the wider society—for instance, from the media.** This is often best done by introducing information that contradicts and complicates thinking in stereotypes, as the classroom examples in this chapter illustrate.

☐ **Rather than feeling you always have to "fix" children's stereotyped ideas or immediately answer all their questions about diversity, focus on helping them express their diverse ideas and provide feedback to**

each other. This can encourage them to share the responsibility of creating an anti-biased classroom and, through their participation, actively build less stereotyped and biased ideas.

A DISCUSSION TO EXPAND GENDER ROLES THROUGH A GIVE-AND-TAKE DIALOGUE

The two examples at the beginning of this chapter show how anti-bias education can be built into the curriculum of Peaceable Classrooms. Here is an example of the kind of give-and-take, problem-solving dialogue you can use around any diversity issue. In this case, a teacher of four-year-olds is working on gender-bias with the children in her classroom.

Text	Commentary
Teacher: I've been noticing something in the classroom that hasn't been feeling so good to me. I've noticed that only boys have been playing in the block area.	• The teacher presents the topic to the class as a problem to be solved. In this sense, she uses the meeting to take the children through a problem-solving sequence similar to the one for resolving conflicts described in the preceding chapter.
You know how we've talked before about how it's important to do all the activities around the classroom.	• She tries to help the children connect to prior experience and knowledge.
I wonder if you have any ideas about this—how come the girls don't choose blocks?	• She immediately gets the children to express their ideas, even if there is a *risk* of responses expressing stereotypes.
Henry: Boys like using blocks more.	• Possible egocentrism. And he focuses on one aspect of the situation only. Also, he seems to be dividing boys and girls up into two dichotomous categories.
Helen: Boys always sign up first. There's never any room in blocks.	• She is making a logical causal connection.

T.: So sometimes when girls want to sign up, the boys have already taken all the spaces on the choice board? I know blocks are really popular with a lot of boys.

- Without judging them, T. elaborates on one child's ideas. In this way she serves as the *intermediary* between the speaker and the other children.

Josh: Yeah. Boys are better.

- He is stating an opinion that may or may not be a stereotype.

T.: You think the boys are better. Can you say more about that? How are boys better?

- T. asks an open-ended question to determine if he's thinking in stereotypes.

Josh: Boys are better in the blocks.

T.: Oh, I see. You think boys are better with the blocks. Does anyone else have anything to say about that?

- T. tries to elicit comments that could lead to contradicting or complicating thinking about a stereotype.

Joyce: They *are* better. The boys use them more so they're better.

- This may not be what T. expected to hear, but it does elaborate on the issue. And it indicates the child's perceptions and sense of causality.

T.: So you think if you use blocks a lot, it helps you get better, and boys use them more than girls. Anyone else?

- T. emphasizes Joyce's *causal connection* between experience and expertise; this might help the girls realize *what they need to do* to get better at blocks.

Sheila: That's 'cause the boys never let us use the blocks.

- Here is another causal connection. Many of these children clearly are comfortable saying what they think.

Jenny: Yeah. They use all the blocks. We never get enough to do what we want. [Several girls nod in agreement, while boys start to mumble objections.]

- Clearly, a lot of tension has built up between the girls and boys over blocks. T. seems to have tapped into a valuable issue for the children to address and work on.

T.: It sounds like some of the girls don't feel very good about going into the block area. Can anyone say more about that?

- T. acknowledges and validates the feelings. While she makes sure the children know she is still in charge and keeping things safe, she is giving them a lot of room to explore and understand the problem.

Kamiko: I never sign up for blocks—boys won't let you build what you want.

- She focuses on one key aspect of the situation.

Henry: They can't do it right. They wreck our buildings. Yesterday they wrecked my marble run. It fell.

- Both boys and girls seem able to provide negative feedback to each other without hurting feelings of individual children.

T.: Well, I can tell from what all of you have said that we do have a problem. You all seem to have complaints about what happens when boys and girls are together in blocks—the girls don't feel very comfortable or safe building when boys are there, and some boys don't feel like things work very well when girls are there. [Most children nod in agreement.]

- T. summarizes the problem and tries to help; the children see it as a shared problem when is it presented from both the girls' and the boys' points of view.

Who has any ideas about what we can do so the boys and girls can both play in the blocks and feel good about it?

- T. now shifts the discussion to finding a *"win-win"* solution that can work for all the children.

Jamal: Both take turns.

- Jamal offers a static idea without any sense of what it might mean in practice.

T.: How would that work?

- T. gets child to elaborate his idea for others.

Jamal: You could have boys use blocks one day and girls use blocks one day.

- The beginning of incorporating two different ideas in a dynamic (rather than static) way.

Karen: Two boys and two girls.

- She is varying Jamal's idea.

T.: That's another way to share. Jamal's idea is that we take turns by having one day when boys go in and the next day when girls go. Karen's idea has two girls and two boys— since four kids can go in blocks at a time, we could have half and half. Any other ideas?

- T. again acts as an *interpreter*, helping the children see their different ideas about how to put a "turn-taking" solution into practice.

Julie: Partners.

T.: Can you say more?

- A potential solution, but it's expressed egocentrically, so other children might not understand what she means.

Julie: Yup. Girl and boy partners to build. They have to build together.

- The teacher's previous efforts to model ways of "working together" with the children has helped them come up with possible solutions here.

Henry: Boys could teach them things.

- Henry clearly likes this solution and has ideas about how it might work. Here he is referring back to the earlier idea that boys are better at blocks and incorporating it into the solution.

T.: You mean partners could help each other learn things—like Henry, you're good at marble runs and Josh, you love towers?

- T. tries to stress the idea of helping others by sharing special skills. This gives the children concrete ideas about how they might successfully work together.

[Several children seem to be nodding approval, but a few also seem to be getting restless. T. decides to speed up.]

- This has been a long discussion for children this age. T. needs to decide how to pace things to take into account the needs and attention spans of all the children.

That last solution reminds me of when we've talked before about ways we can teach each other new things. Raise your hand if it feels okay to try having partners. [Most children raise their hands.]

- T. decides to go with this solution. She bases her choice on the apparent interest of many of the children in this solution, and she checks with the children to make sure they agree this is a "win-win" solution.

Okay. We'll try partners. But let's make sure we check in with each other in a few days to see how it's working. We need to stop now, but tomorrow, before sign-up time, we'll talk about how to choose partners.

- Before they end, T. makes sure the children know what comes next in this problem-solving process—how to translate the solution into practice.

ANTI-BIAS EDUCATION IS AT THE HEART OF EDUCATION FOR WORLD PEACE IN THE EARLY YEARS

Infusing anti-bias education into all aspects of the Peaceable Classroom poses an enormous challenge. Society and the children in early childhood settings are more diverse than ever before. As discussed, young children are predisposed to interpret similarities and differences among people in sterotyped ways. Add to this the fact that from very early in life children are exposed to many examples of racism, sexism, classism, and other stereo-types, as well as vast amounts of violent imagery, both real and pretend. This teaches that differences among people are justifiable cause for vio-lence. Only very recently has anyone even begun to work out what develop-mentally appropriate anti-bias education might look like, and there is still a lot more to learn. And, perhaps even more than with any other aspect of Peaceable Classrooms, effective anti-bias education requires that you con-tinually forge new responses and approaches based on the immediate demands and needs of your particular group of children.

Yet, for children to become truly responsible and caring members of a global community where diverse people cooperate and resolve conflicts peacefully, a foundation needs to be laid early. It is the ideas about similari-ties and differences that children construct in the early years upon which all later ideas on the subject must be built. And, it is through helping young children develop critical thinking skills about justice and diversity, learn to respect and stand up for themselves and others in the face of injustice, and come to a just and comfortable relationship with diversity among people, that they will develop the strategies they need to break the cycle of violence in their own lives and in the wider society.

Chapter 7

FACILITATING PLAY: COMBATING THE NEGATIVE INFLUENCE OF VIOLENT MEDIA AND MEDIA-LINKED TOYS*

HALLOWEEN PLAY

On Halloween in this class of four-year-olds, many children came to school in costumes. Out of ten boys, seven are dressed up, four as Teenage Mutant Ninja Turtles (TMNT). Of ten girls, eight dressed up, four as the Little Mermaid. Two of the four TMNT are Spanish-speaking and not fluent in English. All of the Turtles have store-bought swords attached to their store-bought costumes.

The Turtles begin running around the room, screaming, "Turtle power!" The Spanish-speaking children are following and imitating the karate chops and "cowabungas" of the English-speaking children. The Little Mermaids are swimming around on the floor in one area of the room and asking if the Turtles want to swim with them in the water. The Turtles join the Mermaids on the floor, pretending to swim around. All seem to be enjoying themselves when one child, who is not in costume, comes over and announces, "I will be a whale swimming in the water with you." Without waiting for an answer, the whale starts to swim around. Then he says, "Now I will eat the Mermaids and Turtles because I am so hungry." All of a sudden, one of the Turtles jumps up, whips out his sword,

*   For a more detailed discussion of many of the issues and ideas raised in this chapter, see N. Carlsson-Paige and D. Levin, *The War Play Dilemma: Balancing Needs and Values in the Early Childhood Classroom*, (New York: Teachers College Press, 1987); *Who's Calling the Shots? How to Respond Effectively to Children's Fascination with War Play and War Toys*, (Philadelphia: New Society Publishers, 1990); and D. Levin and N. Carlsson-Paige, "Television for (not against) Children: Developmentally Appropriate Programming," *Young Children* (in press).

starts karate kicking the whale, and yells, "You can't eat me. I am a Ninja Turtle, Leonardo. I will fight you!" Now, the other Turtles pull out their weapons, and all gang up on the whale. The Mermaids, with loud screeches, run away from the scene. At first it looks as if the whale and TMNT are play fighting, but soon the little boy who is the whale cries out in defense, "I was only play-ing, I wasn't really going to eat the Turtles." A teacher comes over, upset that yet another dramatic play episode involving Turtles has ended with fists and tears. As the little whale begins to sob, the TMNT all jump in, saying, "We were only playing."

CHANGES IN PLAY: FROM PLAY TO IMITATION

Media is playing a greater and greater role in children's lives. Not only do many children have less time to play than children used to, but also when they do have time, their play is highly influenced by the media. *What they play*, as illustrated by the TMNT/Little Mermaid scenario, is more highly influenced by what they have seen on the screen. How they play and what they play with are also often controlled by the media. Whole lines of realistic toys (like the TMNT costumes and swords) are marketed to accompany TV shows and movies, channeling children into acting out the salient aspects of the shows. Add to this videogames like Nintendo—where the bulk of toy-buying dollars are now going and the vast majority of which are violent. Although they are *called* toys, they promote little, if any, constructive play. Media also influence *what children are learning as they play* and much of that is highly gender-stereotyped—for instance, girls modeling themselves after the helpless, sweet, and pretty Little Mermaid and boys imitating the fighting and machismo of the TMNT and X-Men. (See Chapter 1 for a more complete discussion on the impact of media on children's play.)

The play scenario described above is not unusual. Teachers all over the country have reported similar episodes of media-influenced play that abruptly ends when someone gets hurt or breaks down into tears.* This apparent change in children's play has serious ramifications for children and teachers.

First, many teachers say they spend more and more time entering into play situations to discipline—rather than facilitate. They spend time setting limits and even redirecting children away from their play, helping hurt and crying children, and mediating disputes among children. With these kinds of problems accelerating, play, which has been viewed for decades as an

---

* The complete findings of this study are reported in N. Carlsson-Paige and D. Levin, "The Subversion of Healthy Development and Play: Teachers' Reactions to the Teenage Mutant Ninja Turtles," *Day Care and Early Education* 19, no. 2 (Winter 1991): 14-20.

Here are examples of the toy boxes of single-purpose, media-linked toys. Coming from the imagination of adults, not children, they are highly violent and seemingly exploit a serious societal problem to capture children's interest in them.

essential part of the fabric of early childhood classrooms, has instead become a problem in many classrooms, something to be avoided.

Second, many children are being deprived of needed opportunities to engage in rich and meaningful play, an essential component of healthy development and growth. In play children use their creativity and imagination to transform experience into something uniquely meaningful for each player. As they do so, their sense of emotional control, mastery, and well-being is enhanced, as is their intellectual understanding.

For play to serve development, every child needs to be in charge of what happens—to be his or her own scriptwriter, director, producer, actor, costumer, set designer, and prop person. For instance, when children play "house," each child brings his or her own unique experiences, needs, concerns, and questions into the play—how and what to prepare for pretend meals, how to talk to each other as they pretend to eat, how to work on disagreements that arise, and how to feed the "baby" (doll). Thus, no two children's house play scenarios should ever look exactly the same.

But media-influenced play can undermine this deeply personal process. For instance, rather than treating the efforts of the "hungry whale" to become involved in their play as a unique and exciting script, adding a new dimension to their play, the Turtles can only focus on the TMNT response they learned to imitate and enjoy most—attacking and fighting with their play swords. As a result, the play quickly deteriorates, one child ends up scared and upset, none of the children gets the wide range of benefits that would have resulted from more sustained and elaborated play, and the "safety rule" has been violated.

Many young children today spend a lot of their play time engaged in this kind of media-influenced imitative play rather than creative play of their own making. Thus, the opportunities for their play to serve their development and learning are seriously diminished. And even more worrisome, children run a serious risk of never learning to create deeply meaningful and growth-producing play.

DEVELOPMENT AND LEARNING ARE UNDERMINDED

- **Intellectual development is threatened when children are deprived of the kind of play that would help them use content from their direct experience to construct new and more advanced ideas and skills.** In addition, as the whole process of play is undermined, so are children's opportunities to develop creativity and imagination, problem-solving skills, the ability to take risks and try out new ideas, and the confidence that they can solve problems and master academic skills on their own.

- **Media-scripted imitative play can seriously impair children's social development.** When children are following someone else's script about how to treat others, they are not engaging in the kind of active, social knowledge building necessary to develop a broad repertoire of increasingly advanced social understandings and skills. Instead, when much of the behavior in the script children are imitating is violent, they cannot help but learn a repertoire of violent and antisocial behavior. Furthermore, because much of the media content children bring to their imitative play contains many gender, racial, and ethnic stereotypes, it leads to mistrust and intolerance about differences among people (see Chapter 6, *Anti-bias Education: Helping Children Understand and Appreciate Diversity*).

- **With respect to emotional development, imitative play offers children few chances to experience the satisfaction and power that can come from working something out in a personally meaningful and creative way.** Being deprived of the deep satisfaction of play can lead children to look outside themselves for satisfaction and make them susceptible to the influence of others—for instance, peers, TV characters, and advertisers. In addition, since elaborated play provides children with endless opportunities to develop a sense of competence and confidence in their ability to affect the world, failure to engage in such play can contribute to a sense of disempowerment and impotence.

FROM BANNING TO FACILITATING PLAY

Because many teachers recognize that play episodes like the Turtle/Mermaid one have little value for children (and can even harm them) and because such episodes can cause such havoc in classrooms, early childhood teachers often have compelling arguments for banning media-controlled imitative play. Yet many of those who try to enforce a "no war and weapons play (or pretend fighting) at school" rule face a constant struggle. Some even say that it can feel as if a guerrilla war has erupted, as children sneak around the room or playground, trying to hide this kind of play from adults or turning their snack crackers into pretend guns and then gobbling them up before they can be accused of violating the "no guns in school" rule.

It is not at all surprising that content from the media is so central to children's play and therefore so hard for teachers to ban. Children bring to their play the most salient and graphic aspects of their experience—the content they are struggling most to work out and understand. But because children usually end up *imitating* the violent parts of media content over and over instead of creatively working out their own solutions and understandings, *the issues they bring to this kind of play are rarely adequately resolved.*

Struggling to ban media-controlled imitative play, or even trying just to contain it, can be appropriate stopgap measures when the problems created by the play become too great. But, for children to work through their deep issues and needs in a meaningful way, they will require much more direct help from adults.*

Implications for Practice:

☐ **Children need help from their teachers in working through the issues raised by violent and disturbing content in the media.**

☐ **Many children also need their teachers' help in learning how to engage in rich and meaningful play that optimally serves their development.**

☐ **Teachers also need to help children use their play to learn a rich repertoire of social skills—for instance, resolving conflicts, cooperating and sharing, perspective taking—for living together nonviolently in a Peaceable Classroom.**

☐ **Children who have experienced violence in their own lives will be the ones who most need play to work out their issues.** Therefore, while it will not be easy, it is especially critical that teachers support and facilitate the kind of play that can help these children meet the social, emotional, and intellectual challenges resulting from their experiences with violence.** We will need support, training, and resources to learn how to do this well.

A CLASS DISCUSSION FACILITATING NONVIOLENT, CONSTRUCTIVE PLAY

At the end of the earlier TMNT/Little Mermaid episode, when the whale dissolved into tears, the exasperated teacher immediately intervened. As soon as she had calmed things down and assured everyone's safety, she helped the children use the positive approach to conflict resolution described in Chapter 5. In addition, because Turtle play was a growing problem for the children and herself, she decided to take a greater role in helping the children work through the problems created by the presence of TMNT in the classroom. To this end, she led the following discussion the next day at circle time:

---

* For a more thorough discussion of the various approaches for dealing with media-influenced fighting play, see N. Carlsson-Paige and D. Levin, *The War-Play Dilemma: Balancing Needs and Values in the Early Childhood Classroom*, (New York: Teachers College Press, 1987).

** For a more detailed discussion of the importance of play as a vehicle for helping young children who have directly experienced violence to heal, see J. Garbarino et al., *Children in Danger: Coping with the Consequences of Community Violence*, (San Francisco: Jossey-Bass, 1992).

Text	Commentary
Teacher: I have been thinking about a problem that's been happening in the classroom, and I need your ideas about how we can solve it.	• The teacher states the problem that will be their discussion topic. • T. makes it clear the children will play a crucial role in solving the problem.
You know how a lot of children have been playing Teenage Mutant Ninja Turtles lately? [Most children enthusiastically nod or call out, "Yes."]	• She tries to get the children to tap into their recent classroom experience with Turtle play. • T. knows there is a lot of interest in Turtles and Turtle play. That's why she wants to try other approaches before discussing a ban on the play.
T.: Well, when you play Turtles, it doesn't feel safe. It seems like almost all they do is fight and pretend to use weapons.	• T. explains the problem in terms of the "safety rule."
And almost every time children start playing Ninja Turtles, it ends up with someone getting hurt or angry or upset.	• She tries to help children see the causal connections between Turtle play and children's not feeling safe.
I don't like that a lot of you are spending so much time pretending to fight.	• T. expresses her opinion about this kind of play without casting blame on the players.
And I don't like it that so many children are getting upset and don't feel safe.	• T. shows why she does not like the TMNT play by citing its concrete effects on children.

I want your ideas about that.

- As soon as T. has explained the problem, she brings the children into the discussion.

Lawrence: Turtles like to fight! They have awesome weapons.

- Lawrence obviously feels comfortable to say exactly what he thinks, not what he thinks T. wants to hear!

Carl: Yup. The nun chuck is the best.

- Like many TMNT lovers, Lawrence and Carl both first focus on the most salient and powerful aspect of the Turtles.

Ted: I'm always Leonardo. I like him most.

- T. lets the boys make their egocentric points without passing judgment.

T.: Anyone else?

- T. takes the time needed to get to other kinds of responses.

Julie: I don't like them. All they ever do is fight.

- This is not an uncommon comment from girls. TMNT play is usually highly gender divided. As in many shows, fighting is reserved for males, and females are helpless and do not like fighting.

T.: Is there anything they like to do besides fight?

- T. remains neutral but tries to help the children expand their thinking beyond "Turtles fight."

Ted: Yeah. Eat pizza.

- This is the most common nonviolent action young children mention for the Turtles because when TMNT are not fighting, they love to eat pizza.

T.: Anything else?

- T. is not looking for a single "right" answer. She wants to help the children express and clarify their ideas.

Chorus: Noooo.

- This effort of refocusing away from violence doesn't get T. very far!

T.: What do you think makes them like to fight so much?

- T. tries a new approach.

Ted: To kill Shredder.

- Shredder is the Turtles' enemy.

Mark: Yeah. Shredder is really, really bad. They need to kill him.

- Like most contemporary children's media bad guys, Shredder is a unidimensional, totally bad character to whom good guys (the TMNT) can do any horrendous thing they want.

Chris: It's bad to kill. You shouldn't kill.

- This child *may* be spouting rote dogma heard from adults or may be struggling to apply to this situation a moral idea he has begun to grapple with.

T.: I wish there were some other things the Turtles could do besides fight—that they could find other ways to solve their problem with Shredder without anyone getting hurt.

- Again, T. states an opinion without blaming children, thereby helping shift the discussion from defining the problem to coming up with a solution.

Mary: They could use their words.

- This, too, could be rote dogma.

T.: Use words. Who has an idea about what they could say? [Brief discussion]

- By asking this question, T. is helping children learn words they can use to avoid fighting with Shredder in their play.

Sandy: They could trick him.

- Another example of children expressing diverse ideas, not "right" answers.

T.: Trick him? How would that work? [Brief discussion]

- T. tries to help the group get the information they need to assess and try out Sandy's idea.

Chris: They could catch him.

Shelly: Yeah! And put him in jail.

- Shelley sees immediate possibilities in this idea.

T.: So you could put him in jail instead of fighting with him.

- T. summarizes this possible solution.

I just wonder how you could catch him without anyone getting hurt—in a way that didn't feel unsafe. [Brief discussion.]

- She helps them anticipate a possible problem if they use this solution.

Those are definitely other things the Turtles could do besides fighting. Maybe the next time you play Turtles you could try some.

- T. summarizes and encourages children to try out their various solutions so they can collect concrete data about how they work.

Let's see how they work, because when you try to kill Shredder, even though it's supposed to be play, it seems hard for you to not end up hurting someone or making someone feel unsafe.

- T. bases her objection to pretend killing on grounds of concrete safety issues, not abstract values, which are harder for young children to understand.

- She sympathizes with the children for their problem rather than blaming them for it.

I have another question. Does Shredder like pizza?

- T. goes in a new direction. It could help humanize the enemy, showing something the TMNT and Shredder have in common.

Adam: Nooooo. He doesn't eat pizza. The Turtles do.

- Children often divide things into rigid, non-overlapping categories.

T.: I wonder what he does like to eat, then. What if you get him in jail? What would you feed him?

- T. accepts Adam's rigidity but keeps trying to make Shredder less unidimensional—i.e., even if he's bad, he eats, as Turtles do.

Sandra: If he was in jail, he'd have to eat pizza.

T.: Look what I have here. [She reaches into a bag and brings out an assortment of miniature plastic food, including tiny pizzas.]

- T. tries to expand the TMNT play beyond its narrow focus on violence by bringing in a realistic but open-ended play material—food. She has chosen food because it came up in the initial conflict, is something the Turtles like, and is common to the experience of all the children.

Adam: Oh boy! We can put Shredder in jail.

- Clearly, T. has excited at least one child about a way to expand his play.

T.: Okay. So today, when you play Turtles, you can make a jail. Who has ideas where it can be? And maybe Shredder and the Turtles will be hungry.

- Because there seems to be little opposition, T. moves right ahead into helping the children plan how to put their solution (making a jail for Shredder and feeding him) into action.

Remember yesterday. *I hope the Turtles and other animals eat the food, not each other, when they get hungry this time!*

- T. ends by explicitly and humorously helping the children connect their prior experience to the new play.

This teacher uses a wide range of key, developmentally appropriate approaches for fostering the children's participation in their Peaceable Classroom (see Chapter 3, *Setting the Stage: The Peaceable Classroom*, and Chapter 4, *Building a Peaceable Classroom Through Give-and-Take Dialogues*). In the process, she also *helps the children discover ways to expand their media-influenced imitative play in more meaningful, less violent directions.*

Implications for Practice:

☐ **Help children elaborate the content of their play beyond its narrow focus on violence. Through such efforts children can regain control of their play.** For instance, with the teacher's help the children in the above discussion got excited about putting Shredder in jail and feeding him, instead of trying to kill him.

☐ **Help children learn to use more open-ended, less realistic toys as props in their play.** By deciding to build a jail out of blocks and use miniature food that is not specific to any TV program and common to the experience of all the children, the teacher helped them get beyond single-purpose media-linked toys and bring more of their own ideas and experiences into the play.

☐ **Work to combat what the children are learning in the media about violence and bringing to their play.** By expressing concern about the children's violent play without condemning it, the teacher helped the children hear the range of views in the class about the Turtles' violence and tried to make the enemy, Shredder, seem less unidimensionally bad. As a result, the children developed slightly more complicated thinking and assimilated ideas and values that could lead them away from a focus on violence. Chapter 11, *Class Puppets*, suggests another way of helping children expand their understanding of violence through meaningful play.

☐ **Provide children with an alternative to the violent content from media by suggesting appealing content for their play.** A rich and meaningful curriculum can offer many starting points for play, as can children's experiences out of school. But in both cases, many children will need your help, especially at first, bringing content from their everyday experience into their play. Chapter 12 offers suggestions for using children's books to provide content that can promote play.

PART II

Practical Ideas for Teaching Peace

INTRODUCTION: STARTING POINTS FOR CURRICULUM DEVELOPMENT IN PEACEABLE CLASSROOMS

As we have seen, Peaceable Classrooms grow out of understanding how children develop ideas about peace, conflict, and violence knowing how to infuse ideas about them into the curriculum and daily classroom life. Once you have constructed this developmental framework, you can begin to look at specific curriculum activities and make informed judgments about whether and how they might contribute to your Peaceable Classroom.

In my work with teachers, I have seen many original and effective Peaceable Classrooms. The richest approaches generally provide enough structure so that children can organize their ideas and actions, but are flexible and open enough so that what happens can evolve and change with you and your children.

In the chapters that follow, I have included a few of the most exciting and powerful approaches I have seen. I have selected them because they can serve as starting points for a curriculum, can be adapted to a variety of settings and ages, and can become powerful tools for organizing what happens in a classroom.

Chapter 8

CLASS GRAPHS: BUILDING COMMUNITY IN PEACEABLE CLASSROOMS

One way to promote peaceable living and learning is to collect meaningful information about the children in the class and represent it on simple graphs the children can "read." This approach can provide a wealth of developmentally appropriate curriculum activities that help achieve the goals of the Peaceable Classroom while incorporating much of the "regular" curriculum of early childhood classrooms, such as foundations for literacy and numeracy.

One teacher used "class graphs" as a regular feature of her kindergarten Peaceable Classroom curriculum. She made a large blank graph on oak tag (approximately 2.5 feet by 4 feet) with four columns and ten rows, marking squares the size of Polaroid photographs. Then she laminated the whole sheet with clear plastic and stuck a piece of Velcro at the top of each square, so that children's laminated photos (which had Velcro on their backs) could easily be stuck onto and taken off of the graph. Figure 2 shows how it looked.

Figure 2
OUR CLASS GRAPH

The Question
of the Day:

10 • • • • • • • • • •				
9 • • • • • • • • •				
8 • • • • • • • •				
7 • • • • • • •				
6 • • • • • •				
5 • • • • •				
4 • • • •				
3 • • •				
2 • •				
1 •				

When children visited the classroom before the start of the school year, the teacher took a Polaroid photograph of each child. Then when they arrived on the first school day, she had the photo ready with each child's name on the bottom, a plastic laminated protective cover, and a piece of Velcro (or magnetic tape) on the back. The children indicated their responses to a question on the class graph by sticking their photos in the column with their choice written and symbolized at the bottom. Throughout the year, the children regularly gathered information about themselves and their diversity in this way and discussed it at class meetings.

WHY USE CLASS GRAPHS?

- The graphs allow children to represent and compare *in concrete, visible ways information about themselves*—who they are as respected and safe individuals within a Peaceable Classroom community. Because of how they think, seeing information organized in this way can help children find meaning and make connections that would be hard to find and make on their own.

- The graphs regularly remind *children of the importance and value of their diversity*—who they are; what they think, feel, like, and do; and how they look.

- The graphs enhance children's *mathematical skills* by helping them *see* numerical information in pictorial form. Graphs make concepts such as "more than," "less than," or "the same as," "a lot" or "a little," "most" or "a few," "how many," "how many more," or "how many less" available to children in concrete and visible ways long before the children can understand them or use them to perform logical or symbolic operations.

- *The graphs foster children's literacy skills.* The sample "Our Class Graphs" in Figures 2-7 in this chapter provide a range of cues that help children who are nonreaders still find ways to "read" the information on the graphs. For instance, by providing icons (simple pictorial representations that accompany each word, category, and number) and writing the children's names underneath their photos, the teacher helps children associate words and letters with meaningful information. And, in keeping with ideas about literacy development that grow out of the whole language or emergent literacy approach, as children learn to "read" class graphs, their actual literacy skills are enhanced.

ADAPTING CLASS GRAPHS TO DIFFERENT AGES AND ABILITIES

- With *preschool children, you may want to start with three-dimensional class graphs*, where children actually use their bodies to represent where they go on the graph (for instance, ask children who like pizza to line up on one side and children who do not like pizza to line up on the other).

- *Older children might get to the point where they can do their own surveys and graphs* in the classroom on a variety of topics, which they share later with the class.

- You can ask children who have begun to write to *write down some mathematical conclusions* about what they have "read" on the graph—for instance, "What is the most common way children get to school?"

IDEAS FOR INFUSING CLASS GRAPHS INTO THE CURRICULUM

Here are several additional examples of how you can use class graphs with young children. The numbers of columns and rows in the graphs vary with the age of the children and the topic graphed.

CLASS GRAPHS TO HELP IN THE TRANSITION FROM HOME TO SCHOOL

A kindergarten teacher used this graph on the first day of school as a way of greeting children when they arrived (see Figure 3). She helped them find and choose the column where they wanted their photo, and then, at circle time, she had a brief discussion using the information on the graph to discuss the different ways children can feel on the first day of school, the things that make them feel that way, and how what happened during the day might affect how they feel now. This approach to starting school established right from the start that:

- the children's feelings and thoughts are important;

- diverse ideas are legitimate and valued;

- other children feel the same way they do (e.g., "I'm not the only one scared");

- the children are part of a community that cares about and takes care of its members.

The teacher returned to the graph at the end of the first week of school to

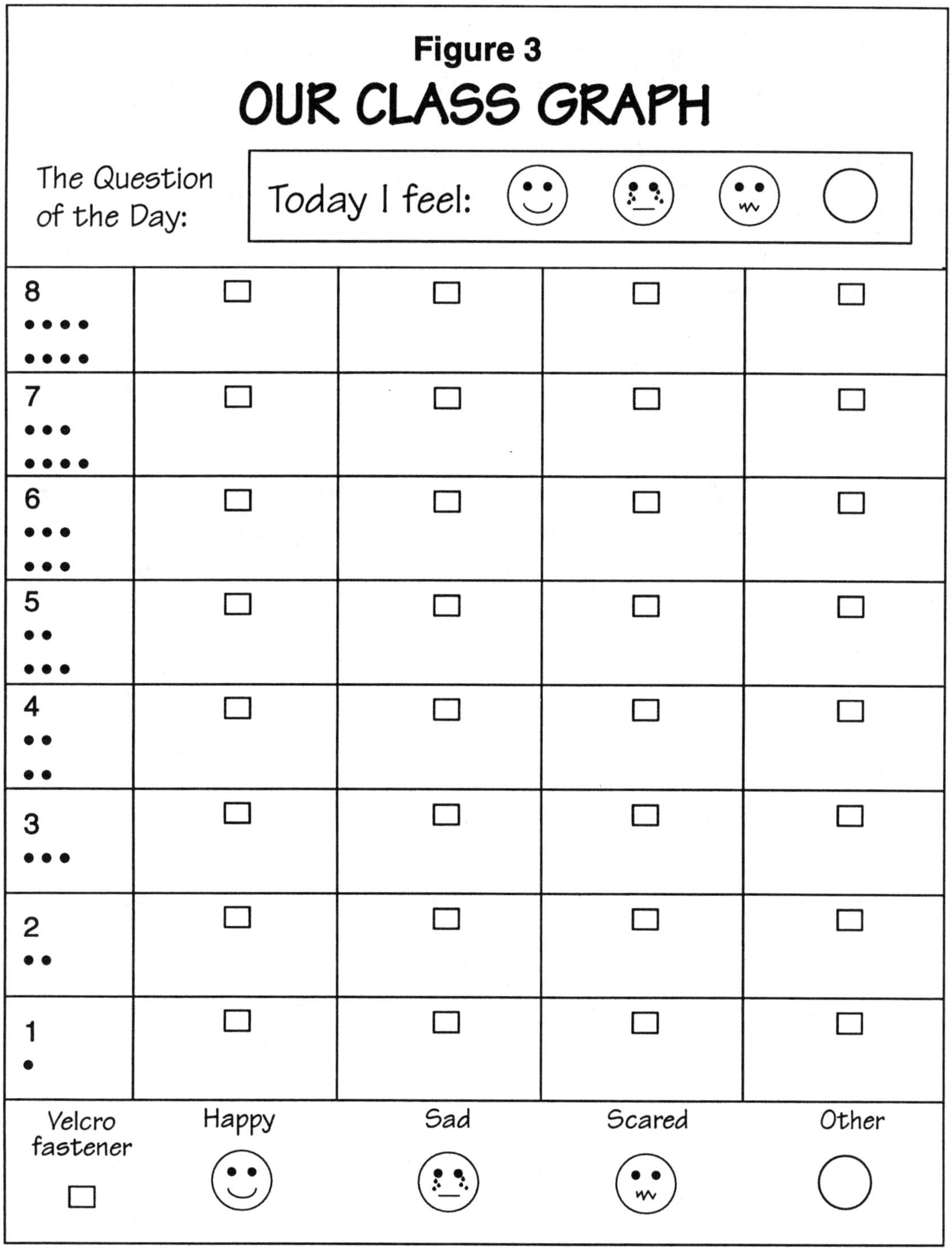

Figure 3
OUR CLASS GRAPH

The Question of the Day:	Today I feel: 😊 😢 😨 ◯			
8 •••• ••••	☐	☐	☐	☐
7 ••• ••••	☐	☐	☐	☐
6 ••• •••	☐	☐	☐	☐
5 •• •••	☐	☐	☐	☐
4 •• ••	☐	☐	☐	☐
3 •••	☐	☐	☐	☐
2 ••	☐	☐	☐	☐
1 •	☐	☐	☐	☐
Velcro fastener ☐	Happy 😊	Sad 😢	Scared 😨	Other ◯

discuss whether any of the children wanted to move their photo because their feelings had changed. Several children eagerly raised their hands.

CLASS GRAPHS TO DEVELOP CURRICULUM AROUND A PERSONALLY MEANINGFUL THEME

One teacher used this graph near the beginning of the year as part of a thematic curriculum unit titled "Getting to Know Us." She developed the unit to help the children with the transition from home to school, to help them feel comfortable with their classmates by discovering things they shared with each other, and to show them they were valued for who they were and what they thought. Each day, the teacher had the children do a graph on a different question about themselves, such as, "How did you get to school today?" (see Figure 4).

Because this teacher introduced graphs at the beginning of the year, the children quickly became comfortable with using graphs as a central part of their daily circle time. Notice that the graph uses simple line drawings of vehicles to help children learn to complete and "read" it independently.

Figure 4
OUR CLASS GRAPH

The Question
of the Day:

How do you get to school?

	Car	Walk	Bus	Subway – T
8	☐	☐	☐	☐
7	☐	☐	☐	☐
6	☐	☐	☐	☐
5	☐	☐	☐	☐
4	☐	☐	☐	☐
3	☐	☐	☐	☐
2	☐	☐	☐	☐
1	☐	☐	☐	☐

This next graph was part of a first grade curriculum unit titled "Our Families." Focusing on numbers of people in the children's families provided an excellent way to discuss different kinds of families—an especially rich topic because the children in the class had many different family constellations (see Figure 5). But even classes without much obvious diversity will still find variations in family size.

Using this graph helped the children work out an understanding of what families are—in a way that promoted a sense of both the similarities and differences among their families. Children also brought in photographs of their families for use in conjunction with graph discussions. Among the math activities that developed from these discussions was one where the children took one Unifix cube (interlocking plastic blocks) for each family member and used the cubes to do calculations like: "What is the total number of people in all the families of the children in the class?" (It took an entire circle time discussion/problem-solving session to work this problem out.) The family puppets described in Chapter 11 provide another rich possibility for curriculum development for this unit.

Figure 5
OUR CLASS GRAPH

The Question of the Day:	How many people are in your family? ♀♀♀♀♀

8	□	□	□	□
7	□	□	□	□
6	□	□	□	□
5	□	□	□	□
4	□	□	□	□
3	□	□	□	□
2	□	□	□	□
1	□	□	□	□
	2	**3**	**4**	**5** → Etc.
	♀♀	♀♀♀	♀♀♀♀	♀♀♀♀♀

CLASS GRAPHS TO HELP FOLLOW UP ON SOLUTIONS TO CLASS PROBLEMS

The graph in Figure 6 was developed as a follow-up activity to the discussion on "what to do when you need help" described in Chapter 4, which resulted in the children's making a "Helper Chart" (see Figure 12) to encourage them to ask each other for help instead of the teacher. About a week after the children made the "Helper Chart," the teacher made this class graph, which asked, "Did anyone ask you for help today?" It was the focus of a follow-up discussion on how well the children thought the chart was working and how they would like to modify it.

Graphs used in this way can provide a wonderful mechanism for *on-going group problem solving*. And the simplicity of graphs with only two columns—for "yes" or "no" answers—makes them well suited for introducing class graphs to very young children.

Figure 6
OUR CLASS GRAPH

The Question
of the Day:

| Did anyone ask you for help today? |

8		
7		
6		
5		
4		
3		
2		
1		

YES — Green   NO — Red

This next graph (see Figure 7) was used to help organize another follow-up discussion. The teacher wanted to check in with the children on how they thought the decision to have girls and boys team up in the block area was working as a solution to boys playing more than girls with the blocks (see the dialogue in Chapter 6). She started with simple yes or no questions on the graph. Was the solution leading to more girls going into the block area? Were children feeling more comfortable with each other when both boys and girls were there? Were there new things they should try?

Figure 7
OUR CLASS GRAPH

The Question
of the Day:

Did you play in the blocks today?

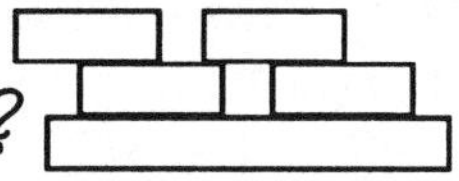

8	☐	☐
7	☐	☐
6	☐	☐
5	☐	☐
4	☐	☐
3	☐	☐
2	☐	☐
1	☐	☐

CLASS GRAPHS TO TEACH
DEMOCRATIC DECISION MAKING

This classroom did a lot of cooking and baking. The children often helped plan menus for what they would prepare for class festivities. Here is a 2-column graph (see Figure 8) the teacher used to take a vote on whether the children wanted to bake cookies or muffins for José's class birthday party.

"Class Graphs" used in this way can provide a developmentally appropriate format for introducing a "democratic" decision-making process (i.e. voting) to young children. It is not as much the idea of voting that is focused on, as the process of participating in collective decision making. In order to build an understanding of a shared decision-making process, young children need many concrete and meaningful opportunities to see how their desires and ideas (i.e., votes) contribute to what actually happens in the classroom. So, do not be too surprised if the voting results are at first treated differently by the children than how you intended to use them. Young children are often more bound by *what they want and whether they get it* than *by what the numbers in the vote say*. And, trying to reach a decision everyone can buy into to some degree still needs to be a central goal even when you introduce voting.

Figure 8
OUR CLASS GRAPH

The Question | What should we bake for Jose's Birthday?:

10 ••••• •••••	☐	☐
9 ••••• ••••	☐	☐
8 •••• ••••	☐	☐
7 ••• ••••	☐	☐
6 ••• •••	☐	☐
5 •• •••	☐	☐
4 •• ••	☐	☐
3 •••	☐	☐
2 ••	☐	☐
1 •	☐	☐

oatmeal cookies   corn muffins

Chapter 9

CLASS CHARTS: BUILDING PREDICTABLE RITUALS, ROUTINES, AND A SENSE OF SAFETY

Young children need help actively learning how cooperative communities work and how to be responsible, contributing members of these communities. This process can be helped immeasurably by establishing predictable and understandable rules, rituals, and routines to guide children's actions in concrete ways. I have seen many teachers use class charts to develop such structures in their Peaceable Classrooms.

USING CLASS CHARTS TO HELP CHILDREN FUNCTION AS AUTONOMOUS LEARNERS AND RESPONSIBLE COMMUNITY MEMBERS

At the beginning of the year, class charts prepared in advance by teachers can help children learn simple things about how to function in their classroom. The "Class Cleanup Chart" (Figure 9), "Choice Board" (Figure 10), and "Our Daily Schedule" chart (Figure 11) are examples of the kind of charts teachers can use from the start of the school year to help children learn to function as autonomous and responsible members of their Peaceable Classrooms. Simple versions of these charts—with names and photos or pictures—can work effectively for children as young as three.

The teachers who made these charts did not expect the children to be able to use them fully at the start. For instance, knowing it is your job to clean up the blocks only has meaning for you when you know exactly what you need to do to clean up the blocks. Choosing the art area on the choice board only has meaning when you know how to use the art materials constructively.

Therefore, helping children learn to use class charts is a vital part of your Peaceable Classroom curriculum during the first weeks of school. I have seen teachers do this in ways that also incorporate the curriculum they are "supposed" to be covering—for instance, reading and math. Each of these beginning-of-the-year charts evolved and changed as the year progressed, based on the issues the children raised once they became fully comfortable with how the charts worked.

"Class Cleanup Chart"

There are many ways to structure the cleanup of a classroom. One way, which can effectively promote a sense of shared responsibility and community in young children, is to use a "Class Cleanup Chart." (Figure 9.) This one consists of two concentric cardboard circles held together at the center by a brass paper fastener. Pairs of children are assigned jobs for a week. Each Monday, the inner circle is moved clockwise by one child's name; so that one child in a pair stays with the same job for the next week with a new partner, and the other child moves on to the next job. This system works extremely well at the beginning of the year because once one child knows a job, a continuous process of teaching it to the next child begins, until all the children have learned all the jobs.

Figure 9

Class Cleanup Chart

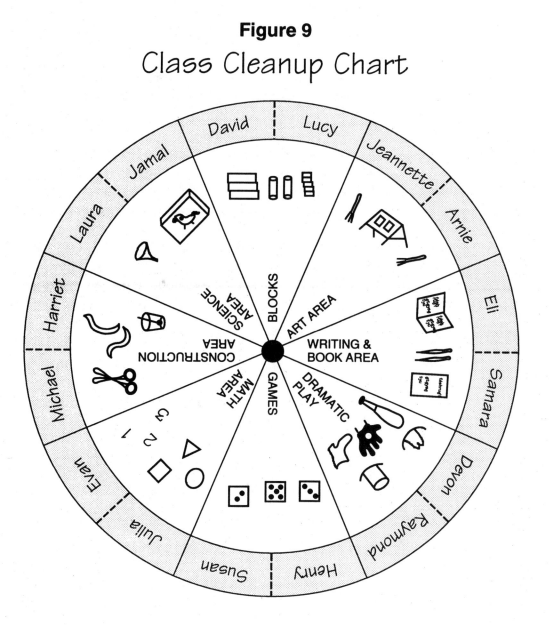

"Choice Board"

The "Choice Board" (Figure 10) is kept in the class meeting area so that children can make their choices at the end of the early morning meeting, when the day's activities and plans are discussed. The little squares on the right are self-adhesive Velcro pieces onto which children can place their personal name circles (stored at the bottom of the board on Velcro fasteners). The number of Velcro squares next to each activity indicates the number of children who can choose that area. The rectangle activity cards on the left, with the activities listed by word and symbol, are also attached to the board with Velcro, so that they can be put on and taken off of the board, depending on what activity areas are open on a given day. Usually an activity card stays up for at least a week, so that all the children trust that they will get a turn, even with very popular activities, and children who get involved with an activity know they will be able to choose it again to continue their work.

FIGURE 10

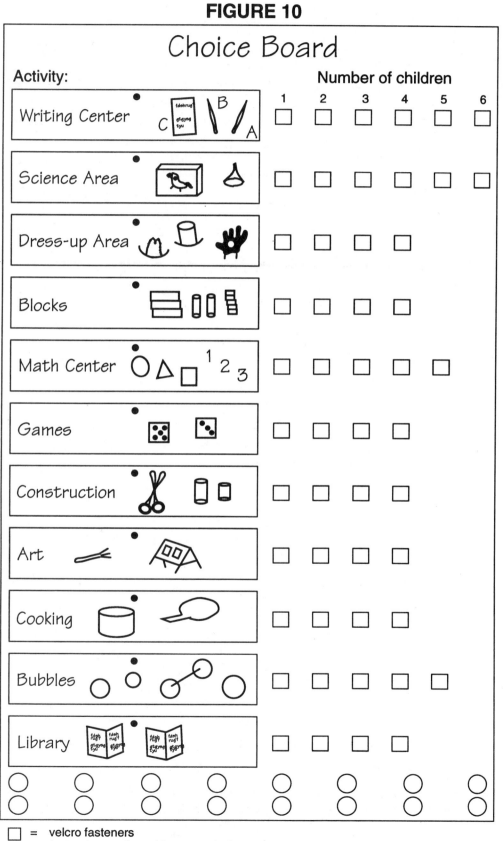

Choice Board

= velcro fasteners
(note: the number of fasteners indicates how many children can go to that area)
= name labels storage area

"Our Daily Schedule"*

The "Our Daily Schedule" (Figure 11) chart represents in words and pictures the fixed sequence of daily activities in a day-care classroom. The column on the right contains information about specific activities that will occur on a given day. The teacher uses self-adhesive magnetic tape to attach cards with special activities to the chart each day (Velcro would also work): what book will be read at class meeting, what fruit will be served at snack, whether a particular child's birthday will be celebrated at lunch, what theme will be set up in the dramatic play area.

This daily schedule chart serves two vital functions:

*   When the children arrive, it provides a *focus for a brief circle time discussion about the day.* Then, the class refers back to it throughout the day as needed, so that the children can learn the rhythm and sequence of their day, know what special activities to expect, and learn to predict when they will be picked up. This is especially reassuring at the beginning of the year, when children need a lot of help finding predictability and order in their day, prerequisites to developing a sense of safety and trust.

*   It greatly *improved communication between school and home and between children and parents* about the children's daily lives in school. The chart was kept near the classroom entrance at the beginning and end of the school day, so that parents could check it and discuss it with their children at drop-off and pickup times.

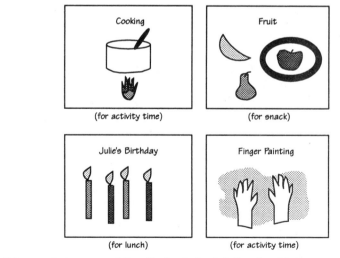

Sample activity cards to go on "Our Daily Schedule" using Velcro.

*   This chart originally appeared in D. Levin and A. Klein, "What Did You Do in School Today?: Using the School Environment to Foster Communication between Children and Parents," *Day Care and Early Education* 15, no. 3 (Spring 1988): 6-10. Reprinted by permission.

FIGURE 11

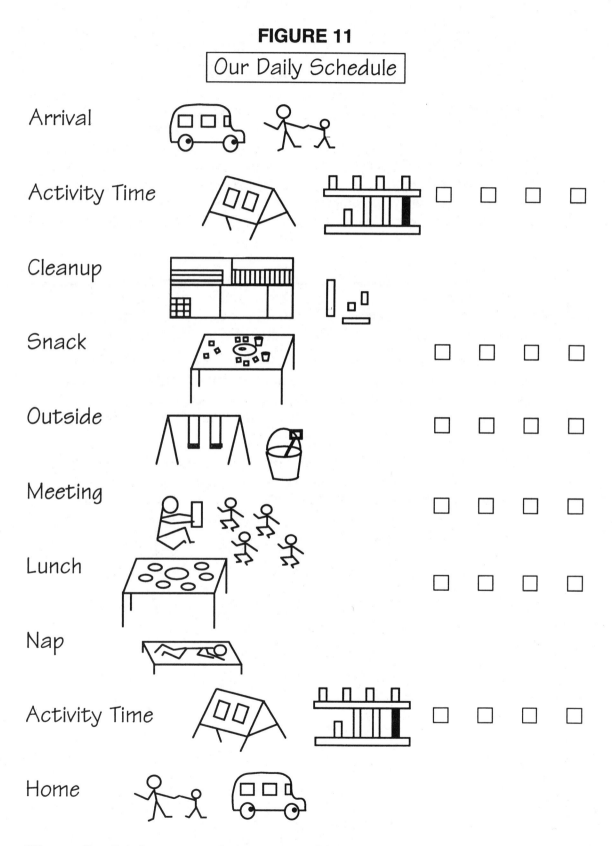

Our Daily Schedule

Arrival

Activity Time

Cleanup

Snack

Outside

Meeting

Lunch

Nap

Activity Time

Home

□ = self-adhesive magnetic tape onto which activity cards with magnetic tape on back can be stuck.

USING CLASS CHARTS TO HELP WITH GROUP PROBLEM SOLVING AND COMMUNITY BUILDING

Class charts can help build a feeling of community, as well as group problem-solving abilities. Brainstorming solutions to a problem or a variety of ways to accomplish something can help children try out new, positive ways of participating in the classroom. Then, by referring back to the charts regularly to build on or modify them based on direct experience, children become involved in the dynamic process of forging their own unique Peaceable Classroom community.

"Helper Chart"

This "Helper Chart" (Figure 12) grew out of the dialogue about getting help in the classroom when the teacher is busy described in Chapter 4, *Building a Peaceable Classroom through Give-and-Take Dialogues*. The categories and names on the chart were developed by the children.

The teacher displayed the "Helper Chart" prominently, so that children could easily remember to use it as the need arose. After about a week, she used the "Did Anyone Ask You for Help Today?" class graph (Figure 6) as the basis for a discussion with the children about how the chart was working and how they might like to change it.

This sequence of activities—1) having a dialogue about a class problem, 2) developing and trying out a solution (the class chart), and 3) using a class graph to discuss how well the solution was working after the children had tried it out—shows how teachers can build a wide range of curriculum activities around Peaceable Classroom goals and issues.

FIGURE 12

Helper Chart

(Who to ask for help)

 • **Counting things**
1 2 3 4
Raymond
Elisha

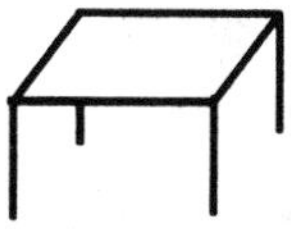

 • **Washing tables**
Jenna
Nathania

 • **Using scissors and glue**
Sam
Darrah
Sally

 • **Hanging up wet paintings**
Tosca
Raymond

 • **Playing hospital**
Sara
Jason

 • **Running**
Kevin
Kendra

 • **Making things in playdough**
Dore
Jenna
Harold

 • **Building with blocks**
Jackson

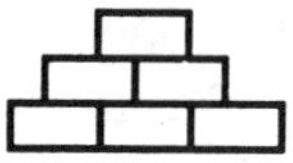

 • **Writing letters in your name**
Sara
Sam
Henry

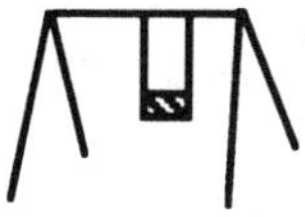

• **Swinging on a swing**
Danielle
Henry

• **Zipping and buttoning (but not tying)**
Jackson
Sally

 • **Washing paintbrushes**
Kendra
Nathania

• **Feeding the gerbil**
Harold
Raymond

• **Drawing Ninja Turtles**
Evan
Jason

"Ways to Be Powerful in the Blue Room"

This chart (Figure 13) was developed by the children in a first and second grade classroom. They redefined what it meant to be powerful. They had been having difficulty resolving conflicts such as who got to play with whom and who used which materials. They were also having problems with teasing and put-downs. To solve these problems, children came up with the items on the chart and discussed ways to put each into practice. They agreed to look out for examples of classmates behaving in these "powerful" ways and were regularly given opportunities to share their observations at meetings.

This group validation of their positive behavior helped the children experience the positive effects of their own (and others') power and built a sense of community and shared responsibility. It provided them a wonderful opportunity to have "power with" rather than "power over" others. In the process of developing and using the chart, classroom and playground behavior improved dramatically.

FIGURE 13

WAYS TO BE POWERFUL IN THE BLUE ROOM

YOU ARE POWERFUL WHEN YOU:

- help each other

- make a new friend

- say you're sorry

- try to get along with each other

- stop a fight

- walk away or ignore someone who is bothering you

- use words (not fists) when you're upset

- share blocks, markers, toys, games

- get help on work or help someone doing work

- do good work

- invite people to play with you

- ask if you can join a group

- help someone who is hurt or sad

BUILDING A CLASS HISTORY WITH A CLASS CHART

Young children only gradually come to realize that history consists of a logical sequence of events connected to the present. They tend to think about *time* in the here and now, where the past is what happened "before now," and the future is what will happen "after now." Yet, to understand how Peaceable Communities work and how they can change in the future, one must first understand how they came to be the way they are now—their history. One powerful, developmentally appropriate way to help children build an understanding of history and time is actually to "build history" with them, using their shared, concrete experiences in their Peaceable Classroom.

To do this, one kindergarten teacher used an ongoing "Class History Chart" (Figure 14). The children counted the number of days they had been at school and built a number line, adding one number each day. Meanwhile, the teacher recorded one special event or activity for each day on a 3-inch by 6-inch file card, on which she wrote a few words and drew a simple picture the children could "read." Then at a daily meeting time, when the children added the number of the day to their number line, they also "read" the "event of the day" card and placed it up with that day's number. Gradually, the special events number line stretched all around the classroom and served as a history of the class' year to which the children could easily refer. On their hundredth day in school, the children had a special celebration, reviewed their class history chart, and reminisced about their accomplishments and how different things felt now from the way they did at the beginning of the number line.

Building a "Class History Chart" in this way helps young children:

- *learn about history and time* in concrete terms they can understand;

- *learn about numbers* in a meaningful context—for instance, how to read and record them and how they are sequenced and "grow";

- *learn literacy skills* as they "read" each day's symbol that is tied to a meaningful experience and then, gradually, figure out the words associated with those symbols;

- experience directly that they are participating members of a caring, cooperative community that has *built a shared history together*.

One teacher used a variation of this "Class History Chart" with three-year-olds. She made a pictorial class history in an album that circulated home, helping create a sense of community among the children, home, and school and giving parents something concrete to talk about with their children.

FIGURE 14

Class History Chart

1	2	3	4	5
Today is our 1st day together.	Today is our 1st day of the Library.	Today is Joanna's Birthday.	Today we baked Pizza.	Today is the end of our 1st week of school.

50	51	52	53	54
Today we counted our pockets. We had 47 pockets.	Today we finished reading "Elmer's Dragon".	Today we ate the pumpkin pie we make. (It was good.)	Today Nanda came back to school with a cast on her leg.	Today Henry's dad came to teach us how to make casts for our fingers.

Chapter 10

CLASS GAMES: PROMOTING COOPERATION, PERSPECTIVE-TAKING, AND A SENSE OF COMMUNITY

Learning to help each other and work together on shared goals is central to living in a Peaceable Classroom. Yet, because of their static thinking, egocentrism, and tendency to think about only one thing at a time, it can be a big challenge for young children to engage successfully with others in give-and-take, cooperative interactions. In the early years, games that loosely structure interactions around a skill or goal help young children learn to engage in give-and-take activities with others. These games can also help counteract the lessons many young children learn when they are exposed too early to competitive games. And the games lend themselves to a holistic curriculum where the content of the games often can relate to a specific subject area, concept, or skill.

"Class games" for young children will not always look like what people commonly call "games." Young children are only just beginning to learn how to use formal rules to guide their behavior with others.* They may realize that rules are used to regulate their own behavior, but they often do not focus on the need for everyone playing a game to follow the same rules or the importance of playing by the same rules throughout the game. And sometimes, even when children can state a rule, translating their words into consistent actions is a very hard next step.

Therefore, it is a challenge to develop class games for young children that not only match their abilities and interests but also promote cooperation and fun rather than competition and misery. You'll need to put aside your adult ideas about games and rules, concepts like winning, losing, competing, and cheating. Pushing children into following rules they cannot yet

---

* For a more complete discussion of how young children learn to understand and use rules, see C. Kamii and R. DeVries, *Group Games in Early Education: Implications of Piaget's Theory*, (Washington, DC: National Association for the Education of Young Children, 1980).

understand can easily lead to rigid, competitive, and stressful participation in games that does nothing to promote the goals of a Peaceable Classroom.

On the other hand, when children do succeed at helping one another accomplish a goal, their ability to participate in a Peaceable Classroom is stretched and strengthened. Working together can help them learn to take into account each other's point of view when deciding how to act. And it can give them the satisfaction of contributing and accomplishing something tangible through working with other children.

Class games for young children rarely have highly structured or complicated rules. Sometimes, when you pick up on and help the children elaborate a give-and-take activity or game they began on their own, the rules originate from the children themselves. At other times, you can give them a starting point for a class game yourself and then help the children adapt and mold it as they play.

However a class game starts, it is often most exciting and valuable when you follow children's leads as their play progresses and help the game develop into a regular and familiar classroom ritual. As you do this, you'll have many opportunities for having periodic give-and-take discussions about such things as:

- what has happened with the game so far;

- the children's ideas about how to continue to expand on and vary the game;

- problems that have arisen and the children's ideas about how to solve them.

"PAIR PAINTINGS": CLASS GAMES STARTED BY CHILDREN

One teacher of four-year-olds reorganized her painting area when she saw two boys create a give-and-take game for painting shared pictures at the easel. The boys were taking turns brushing paint strokes onto a large piece of paper, adding onto each other's lines. Each time one added a stroke, he chanted, "Now this goes on yours." They repeated this process over and over, back and forth. As they continued painting, they speeded up their strokes and chants, and several other children came to watch. The teacher and observers began to chant with the painters.

When the two boys finished their *cooperative painting*, the teacher quickly made more room around the easel, so that other pairs of children could work at it together. All morning, pairs of children used the boys' approach to paintings. Over the next several days, the easel was constantly in use by children developing variations on the "pair painting" game, including:

- chants and actions that focused on

  - color ("Now I'm putting black on yours." "Now I'm putting blue on yours.");

  - specific kinds of brush strokes ("Now here goes a dot." "Now here goes a circle.");

- back-and-forth chants sung to familiar tunes;

- efforts to represent real objects ("Now here goes an eye on the face." "Now here goes a mouth on the face.");

- paintings and chants where three or more children participated.

The teacher regularly asked children to share at class meetings how they had made their pair paintings. With her help, they showed the paintings, describing how they had worked together, and recited the chants they used. Thus, not only were these children gaining experience with give-and-take actions when they painted, the teacher was also helping them see that their efforts to work together toward unique ideas were valued. At the same time, by sharing their painting techniques, they were giving each other new ideas to try when they next did pair paintings at the easel.

Gradually, the idea of working together in pairs spread to other areas of the classroom.

- Some children tried paired block building, where children took turns adding blocks to a building.

- Several used the give-and-take approach at cleanup time, alternating putting objects like blocks back on the shelf.

- Each time the children came up with a new use of the pair game the teacher would ask them to tell about it at a class meeting.

Thus, while the teacher could never have predicted where the pair paintings would lead, it became a central theme or ritual for organizing the social interactions and curriculum in that Peaceable Classroom. And as the children played their pair games, they were also developing language and representational skills, as well as such concepts as logical causality, reciprocity, and color mixing.

BEANBAG GAMES: CLASS GAMES STARTED BY THE TEACHER*

One kindergarten teacher used beanbags to introduce a teacher-guided class game to her children. She made enough beanbags (approximately 3 inches by 3 inches) for every child in her class. First, at class meeting she gave each child a beanbag to try to balance on his or her head. Sitting and balancing was not too hard for the children, but walking around posed a major challenge. Several children became frustrated over how often their beanbags fell. So the children had a brief discussion and decided to help each other learn to balance the beanbags.

The next day, the teacher grouped the children in pairs. One pair member balanced the beanbag, while the other coached the first child about how to walk and returned the beanbag to the "balancer's" head when it fell. Then the children switched roles. The give-and-take of children coaching each other required that the coach learn to de-center and pay attention to the actions and needs of the balancer. Each pair member had an opportunity to experience both needing and giving help. And the children saw the impressive progress they made learning to balance the beanbags.

The children asked to play this class game regularly and seemed to enjoy their growing mastery of balancing beanbags on their heads. Several variations of the "beanbag helper game" evolved including:

- trying to move at varying speeds—from slow motion to fast;

- using a variety of motions while the beanbag is on a child's head—hopping on two feet and one foot, standing on one foot and on tiptoes, and trying to move from standing to sitting and vice versa;

- trying to balance the beanbags on other parts of the body, such as shoulders, knees, and feet;

- first counting and then using a timer to see how long you can keep the beanbag on a child's head;

- trying to balance other things on children's heads, such as mittens (a good item to start with for children younger than five), small blocks, and stuffed animals.

---

* The idea of using beanbags for class games grows out of the "frozen bean-bag game" described by W. J. Kreidler in *Elementary Perspectives: Teaching Concepts of Peace and Conflict*, (Cambridge, MA: Educators for Social Responsibility, 1990). The variations offered here for use with young children can serve as a model for adapting many of the games and activities suggested by Kreidler to Peaceable Classrooms with younger children.

Because of the children's continuing interest in beanbag games, the teacher eventually introduced the "frozen beanbag game." Though still grouped in pairs, all the children had their own beanbags with both children in a pair trying to balance their beanbags at once. When a beanbag fell off one child's head, that child had to freeze until the other child bent down (without dropping his or her own beanbag!) and returned the fallen beanbag to its rightful place. If, as often happened, both children in a pair dropped their beanbags, they both froze. The game continued until everyone was frozen (which did not take very long when the game was first introduced). Later, the class decided that two children would be specially designated as "defrosters." It was their job to return the bean-bags to frozen partners' heads, thereby keeping the game going indefinitely.

The children's idea of adding the defroster role to their game illustrates clearly how class games can encourage children to find better and better ways to help each other succeed. This contrasts with so many of the games children play outside of Peaceable Classrooms that involve finding better ways to compete with each other.

The frozen beanbag game added an exciting new give-and-take interaction to the children's repertoire. It also created a special challenge by *requiring each child to think about at least two things at once*: "What is happening to my beanbag and my partner's beanbag?" *and* "What do I need to do to keep my beanbag balanced on my head while I bend down to get my partner's beanbag and put it back on my partner's head?" And, as they worked on questions like these, the children were also experimenting with such science concepts as cause and effect, gravity, and balance.

Implications for Practice:

☐ **Watch the children to get ideas for activities you can help them develop into class games.**

☐ **At class meeting or small-group times, introduce new group games that can evolve as the children play.**

☐ **Consult curriculum and activity guidebooks for starting points for new games you can adapt to the needs and goals of your Peaceable Classroom.** See Chapter 14, *Additional Resources,* for a bibliography.

☐ **Do not worry about the children following the "rules" of a game too closely**; rather, help them adapt and change the rules as they play.

☐ **Develop games that promote cooperation, collaboration, and fun rather than competition, winning and losing, and wounded feelings.**

☐ **Follow the children's lead as their play progresses to help them further develop their games.**

☐ **Use the children's suggestions for changing a game as occasions for shared decision making.**

☐ **When children have a problem succeeding at a game, take advantage of the chance to support their efforts to learn how to help each other succeed.**

☐ **Make a few class games into regular classroom rituals**; this can help the children develop a sense of predictability, shared experience, and community.

CREATING YOUR OWN CLASS GAMES

Pair paintings and paired beanbag games are two examples of teachers helping children turn small classroom events into long-term and meaningful learning activities. Rarely will it matter what the specific games are; what really matters is the give-and-take interactions that evolve.

Once you begin looking for starting points for class games, you are likely to find that the possibilities are endless. The children will usually be your greatest resource. But many curriculum guides and manuals also provide ideas for games and activities that you can adapt to support the aims of class games described here. (See Chapter 14, *Additional Readings and Resources*.)

Chapter 11

"CLASS PUPPETS":*
PROMOTING PROBLEM SOLVING,
CONFLICT RESOLUTION, AND
COOPERATIVE LEARNING

Puppets provide another concrete and visible way to teach young children vital skills for actively participating in a Peaceable Classroom. You can use them to work on many of the same issues and content you might discuss using give-and-take dialogues.

USING "US" PUPPETS TO ACT OUT EXPERIENCE

Simple puppets of each child in your class (and yourself and other adults, too) can be used to dramatize stories about themselves, their classmates, and their shared class experiences. One teacher made "Us" puppets by taking a full-body photograph of each child, cutting out the child's form, and mounting it on a tongue depressor. Or children can make little self-portraits to glue to sticks (it may be hard to recognize the self-portraits of young children, but that is okay). Using puppets, young children can gradually learn to act out and work on simple scenarios from their experience. They use the puppets to:

- **recreate positive class experiences with each other;**

    Children can use their "Us" puppets to act out something they enjoyed doing together in the classroom. Even young children will enjoy having their own puppet sing favorite songs, "read" familiar books, or pretend to eat a meal. Older children will want to act out more detailed scenarios interacting with other

---

* "Class puppets" are an adaptation for younger children of the "problem puppets" developed by W. J. Kreidler for elementary school age children. Kreidler discusses problem puppets in *Creative Conflict Resolution: More Than 200 Activities for Keeping Peace in the Classroom*, (Glencoe, IL: Scott, Foresman, 1984). For other ways of using puppets and storytelling with young children see the description of "personna dolls" in L. Derman-Sparks et al., *The Anti-Bias Curriculum: Tools for Empowering Young Children*, (Washington, DC: National Association for the Education of Young Children, 1989) and the account for using dolls to create stories about diversity in L. Derman Sparks and K. Taus, "We're Friends: Understanding Diversity Through Storytelling," *Pre K Today* 4, no. 3 (November-December 1989): 40-46, 60.

children's puppets—for instance, dramatizing a recent in-class birthday party or a field trip.

- **act out successful problem-solving and conflict resolution situations**;

    When children successfully work out a problem or conflict, they can recount the experience with puppets as a way to help their classmates learn more about problem-solving and as a means of sharing their successes with others. With young children, it often works best to tell the story yourself as the children move their puppets to act out the story (to the extent that they are able). Gradually, they can begin to fill in pieces of the story on their own and with your help build up to telling the whole story themselves.

- **reenact conflicts and interpersonal problems and try out proposed solutions**;

    Puppets can act out both conflicts the children have actually had and pretend conflicts from books or made up by you to work on a particular issue. At first, you will need to help the children use the puppets to reenact conflicts and problems, filling in crucial information and engaging the children in give-and-take dialogue about the conflict. For instance, after a puppet says something, you can turn to the children to see if they agree or to ask them what the puppet might have said or done instead. You can also ask the children for ideas to help a puppet solve a problem and then have the puppet react to their ideas.

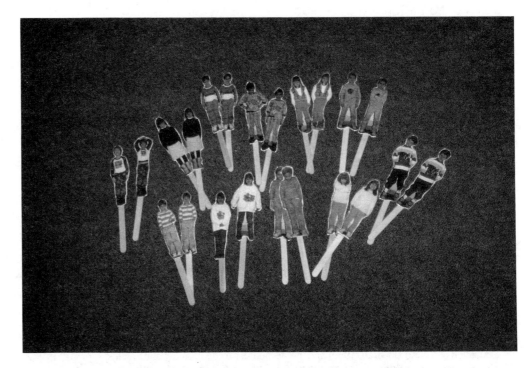

Here are the "Us" puppets from one group of second graders. The children made two puppets each so they could try out different feelings and roles.

"US" PUPPETS PROMOTE THE GOALS OF PEACEABLE CLASSROOMS

When used to work on these kinds of in-class experiences, "Us" puppets provide young children with a meaningful and safe way of learning to live and work together in a Peaceable Classroom. They help children:

- *reenact a wide range of their concrete experiences with others*, both positive and negative, in order to deepen their understanding, skill, and sense of control and mastery;

- *feel they belong to a community* that cares about how people treat each other and values working together on conflicts and problems;

- *reenact their conflicts or problems* once they have calmed down so they can develop new ways of understanding and solving them;

- *try out one or more solutions* to a conflict or problem, get a sense of how that solution feels, and then decide whether they really want to try it out;

- *talk about a difficult situation with others* in a concrete and direct way that avoids the high stakes and emotions of real-world interactions;

- *experience control and mastery* as they distance themselves from real-life situations that may have felt threatening when they happened;

- *develop confidence and skill* with the whole process of trying out ideas, taking risks, and listening to others;

- *get vicarious satisfaction and emotional release* by expressing ideas, feelings, and behaviors that might not be acceptable in real life—for instance, aggression, anger, silliness.

"US" PUPPETS MATCH CHILDREN'S DEVELOPMENTAL LEVEL

"Us" puppets also can help young children expand and complicate their thinking and further develop cognitive skills for solving problems and conflicts peacefully and working together cooperatively. For instance, by working with puppets, children can be helped to:

- move from static thinking about experiences to *more dynamic thinking*, as they use the puppets to transform and vary a given event over and over;

- move from seeing one aspect of a situation at a time *to seeing many aspects* and from seeing isolated parts of a situation to seeing *a more integrated whole*, as they use the puppets to *organize events into a logical sequence* and *make logical causal connections* between them;

- shift from seeing only one point of view (usually their own) to seeing *more than one viewpoint* and even how two viewpoints interact with one another, as they see their various roles and perspectives played out in a nonthreatening situation.

ADDITIONAL IDEAS FOR USING CLASS PUPPETS IN PEACEABLE CLASSROOMS

Once children become comfortable using "Us" puppets, there are many other meaningful ways to incorporate puppets into your Peaceable Classroom.

- **Puppets of favorite book characters**. Using the tongue depressor technique described above, you can make puppets of the characters in your children's favorite stories. Children can then act out parts or all of a story. Younger children will probably just enjoy imitating simple actions and sounds of one character puppet at a time.

- **Puppets of children's favorite media characters**. Puppets of favorite TV and movie characters can help children actively transform what they have seen in the media into something meaningful to them. In addition, the children can use puppets to move the content TV gives them for the characters away from the usual violence, stereotyping, and predictable, simplistic plots. Such puppets can help children get beyond the imitative play that often results from using the highly realistic toys that accompany the shows.

  Using media puppets can also give you insight into what meanings children are making from the shows they watch. With this information, you can begin to develop curriculum activities and give-and-take dialogues that help to modify the meanings children have made.

  One teacher of four- and five-year-olds made puppets of the Teenage Mutant Ninja Turtles with the children and used them to work on the narrow content from the Turtles that children were bringing to the classroom. Another teacher of first-graders made *Wizard of Oz* puppets with her children and used them to recreate the children's favorite parts of the movie.

- **Puppets of the children's families**. Children can also make simple puppets of family members and use them to reenact important experiences at home. Small photos of family members glued to tongue depressors work wonderfully, especially with younger children, but simple drawings can also work well.

Here are child-made family puppets from a second grade class.

Family puppets can be especially valuable for children when some milestone occurs in the family. For instance, when a new sibling is born, the child can use puppets to work on feelings about the new baby and figure out positive ways he or she might interact with the baby. Family puppets can also help build home-school connections for children and can supplement curriculum on diversity among the children's families.

Guidelines for Using Class Puppets with Children

☐ **Children need a lot of help from you in learning how to use puppets productively and nonviolently.** Often, the first thing a child does with a puppet—especially if it fits over the hand—is to punch others with it. Be prepared to teach appealing alternative behaviors.

☐ **Start simply and use the puppets yourself at first, modeling the kinds of things children can do with them.**

☐ **Provide or make the first puppets yourself.** Children need to know something about what a puppet is and what it can do before they are ready to make one themselves.

☐ **Start with simple, small puppets that are less likely to suggest fighting or aggression (as puppets that cover the hand often do).** For instance, as suggested above, use small cutout cardboard figures glued to wooden tongue depressors or craft sticks. Later, old socks with buttons sewn on for eyes can also make simple, appealing, and open-ended puppets.

☐ **Start by working on issues that are not highly emotional or volatile.** In this way, children can develop skills for using puppets before they bring strong emotions into the act.

☐ **In their work with the puppets, encourage the children to tap into the wide range of skills they are learning from their give-and-take dialogues.** For instance, try getting the puppets to use words children have learned, brainstorming solutions to problems or engaging in give-and-take interactions with other puppets.

☐ **Bring in a wide range of issues that show children the rich possibilities of class puppets.**

☐ **Gradually increase children's opportunities to use familiar puppets without your help—individually and in small groups.** For instance, leave the puppets in a designated area in the classroom where children are free to go to play with them in an open-ended way or to work on a problem that has come up for them.

Chapter 12

CHILDREN'S BOOKS: ENRICHING AND EXPANDING THE CONTENT OF THE PEACEABLE CLASSROOM CURRICULUM

WHY USE CHILDREN'S BOOKS?

Children's books can supplement the curriculum of Peaceable Classrooms.* For instance, they can:

- suggest *content for discussions* about the Peaceable Classroom issues you and the children are working on;

- bring into the classroom *content that expands the children's horizons beyond their immediate experience and exposes them to the wide range of diversity* among people beyond the home or school;

- *raise a difficult or potentially loaded issue for discussion* in a way that distances the children from it and makes it seem less threatening;

- provide *content for play* that substitutes for the content children bring to their play from television;

- offer children *specific information and ideas* that expand their understanding and behavior around Peaceable Classroom issues—for instance, by suggesting a new way to think about or solve a conflict;

- help you *interconnect various curriculum areas and goals*—for instance, books foster literacy in children, even as you use them to work on specific Peaceable Classroom content.

---

* For a more complete discussion of using children's books in the curriculum, see N. Carlsson-Paige and D. Levin, "'Wild Things' Not War Things: Using Children's Books to Foster Dramatic Play," in *Who's Calling the Shots*, (Philadelphia: New Society Publishers, 1990) and J. Davidson, "Literature as the Catalyst for Dramatic Play," in *Dramatic Play and Emergent Literacy: Natural Partners*, (New York: Delmar, in press).

Guidelines for Using Children's Books:

There are many ways you can work to enhance the role and impact of children's books in the curriculum:

☐ **Make children's books a regular and valued part of your school day.** Establish such predictable structures and routines as the same "reading aloud" time every day, a place for displaying and storing familiar and currently popular books so that they are readily available to children, a safe and comfortable place where children can look at books on their own or in small groups, some mechanism for children to borrow favorite books overnight or bring in favorite books from home to share with others, and regular communications with parents about special books the class is reading.

☐ **Have regular give-and-take discussions about books you read aloud to the group.** To the extent possible, plan how you will start the discussion based on the issues you feel the book will raise for the children.

☐ **Help children bring the content from popular books into other aspects of the curriculum.** For instance, you might help children build a boat in the block area to go on pirate adventures like Shirley's in *Come Away From the Water, Shirley* by John Burningham. Or you might bring a wheelchair to the classroom for the children to use after reading *Arnie and the New Kid* by Nancy Carlson.

☐ **Read books that seem most meaningful to the children more than once, even many times.** The familiarity that comes from multiple readings can help young children get beyond the more obvious aspects of the book's content and look for deeper and more complex connections and meanings. It can also help the class develop shared meanings and ways of talking about issues together.

☐ **Read more than one book about the same issue, so that children can see the variety of ways that issue can be presented and handled.**

☐ **Read a book and its sequel or a series of books with the same characters.** This can help children get to know a particular character better and try out what has been learned about that character themselves.

☐ **Find ways to use familiar or currently popular books in new ways to support the curriculum and goals of your Peaceable Classroom.** Every book can be used in many different ways, so choosing your books from a specific list, like the one below, is often much more work than thoughtfully adapting the quality books you currently use in the service of your Peaceable Classroom goals.

A SELECTION OF CHILDREN'S BOOKS TO USE IN A PEACEABLE CLASSROOM CURRICULUM

Aardema, V. *Why Mosquitoes Buzz in People's Ears*. New York: Dial Books for Young Readers, 1975.

_____. *Who's in Rabbit's House?* New York: Dial Books for Young Readers, 1977.

_____. *Bimwili and the Simwi*. New York: Dial Books for Young Readers, 1985.

_____. *Rabbit Makes a Monkey of Lion*. New York: Dial Books for Young Readers, 1989.

Aitken, A. *Ruby: The Red Knight*. Scarsdale, NY: Bradbury Press, 1983.

Bach, O. *The Biggest Sneeze*. New York: Caedmon, 1986.

Baer, E. *This is the Way We Go to School: A Book about Children Around the World*. New York: Scholastic, 1990.

Blos, J. *Old Henry*. New York: William Morrow, Mulberry Books, 1987.

Burningham, J. *Mr. Gumpy's Outing*. New York: Thomas Y. Crowell, 1970.

_____.*Come Away from the Water, Shirley*. London: Picture Lions, 1977.

_____. *Aldo*. New York: Random House, 1991.

Burnett, R. *Friends in the Park*. New York: Checkerboard Press, 1992.

Carle, E. *The Grumpy Ladybug*. New York: Viking, Penguin, 1977.

Carlson, N. *Arnie and the New Kid*. New York: Puffin Books, 1990.

Counsel, J. *But Martin!* London: Picture Corgi Books, 1984.

DePaola, T. *Now One Foot, Now the Other*. New York: Trumpet Books, 1981.

Dobrin, A. *Josephine's Imagination*. New York: Scholastic, 1973.

Erikson, J., and M. Roffey. *I Can Share*. New York: Scholastic, 1985.

Foreman, M. *Moose*. New York: Viking, Penguin, 1973.

_____. *War and Peas*. New York: Thomas Y. Corwell, 1974.

Guach, P. *Dance, Tanya*. New York: Scholastic, 1989.

Havill, J. *Jamaica Tag-along*. Boston: Houghton Mifflin, 1989.

Heide, F.P., and J.H. Gilliland. *Sami and the Time of the Troubles*. New York: Clarion, 1992.

Heine, H. *Friends*. London: Picture Lions, 1982.

Henkes, K. *Chrysanthemum*. New York: Greenwillow Books, 1991.

Hoban, R. *Tom and the Two Handles*. New York: Harper and Row, 1965.

_____. *A Bargain for Frances*. New York: Thomas Y. Crowell, 1970.

Hoffman, M. *Amazing Grace*. New York: Dial Books for Young Readers, 1991.

Hughes, S. *Up and Up*. London: Picture Lions, 1979.

_____. *Alfie Gives a Hand*. London: Picture Lions, 1983.

Hutchins, P. *The Doorbell Rang*. New York: William Morrow, 1986.

Isadora, R. *Ben's Trumpet*. New York: William Morrow, Mulberry Books, 1979.

_____. *At the Crossroads*. New York: Greenwillow Books, 1991.

Jones, M. *I'm Going on a Dragon Hunt*. New York: Viking, Penguin, 1988.

Keats, E.J. *Louie*. New York: Scholastic, 1975.

_____. *The Trip*. New York: Scholastic, 1978.

_____. *Regards to the Man on the Moon*. New York: Four Winds Press, 1981.

Keller, H. *Furry*. New York: Greenwillow Books, 1992.

Kellogg, S. *Won't Somebody Play with Me?* New York: Dial Books for Young Readers, 1973.

_____. *The Mysterious Tadpole*. New York: Dial Books for Young Readers, 1977.

Lioni, L. *Swimmy*. New York: Alfred A. Knopf, 1963.

Little, L.J., and E. Greenfield. *I Can Do It by Myself*. New York: Thomas Y. Crowell, 1978.

MacDonald, M.R. *Peace Tales: World Folktales to Talk About*. Hamden, CT: Linnet Books, 1992.

McKissack, P. *Flossie and the Fox*. New York: Dial Books for Young Readers, 1986.

_____. *Mirandy and Brother Wind*. New York: Alfred A. Knopf, 1988.

McLerran, A. *Roxanboxen*. New York: Puffin Books, 1991.

McPhail, D. *Great Cat*. New York: E.P. Dutton, 1982.

_____. *Lost*. New York: Trumpet Books, 1990.

Mendez, P. *The Black Snowman*. New York: Scholastic, 1989.

Myers, W.D. *Mr. Monkey and the Gotcha Bird*. New York: Delacorte, 1984.

Piers, H. *Long Neck and Thunder Foot*. New York: Viking, Penguin, 1982.

Scieszka, J. *The True Story of the Three Little Pigs*. New York: Scholastic, 1989.

Sendak, M. *Where the Wild Things Are*. New York: Harper and Row, 1963.

Seuss, Dr. [T. Giesel]. *The Sneeches and Other Stories*. New York: Random House, 1961.

_____. *The Lorax*. New York: Random House, 1971.

_____. *The Butter Battle Book*. New York: Random House, 1985.

Steptoe, J. *Stevie*. New York: Harper Trophy, 1969.

Swope, S. *The Araboolies of Liberty Street*. New York: Clarkson N. Potter, 1989.

Udry, J.M. *Let's be Enemies*. New York: Harper and Row, 1961.

Williams, V. *Cherries and Cherry Pits*. New York: William Morrow, Mulberry Books, 1986.

Winthrop, E. *That's Mine*. New York: Holiday House, 1977.

Wood, A. *Heckedy Peg*. New York: Harcourt Brace Jovanovich, 1987.

Chapter 13

CURRICULUM WEBS: PLANNING AND KEEPING TRACK OF CURRICULUM ON A THEME OR TOPIC

Planning and keeping track of curriculum activities that are tailored to all your children's needs and backgrounds, developmental levels, and current experiences poses challenges you would not have to face if you followed a prescribed curriculum. To develop an effective Peaceable Classroom curriculum requires careful organization; keeping track of the overall functioning of the classroom, each activity's progress, and each child's needs, performance, and progress; while making constant decisions about what comes next and how to build it on what came before.

In addition, this more open-ended, child-centered, nonlinear approach can present many pitfalls for a teacher. It is never certain where an activity will go. One topic often flows into the next. Subject areas do not always fit into distinct compartments or activities. Each child contributes and learns ideas and skills unique to him or her, and there are few predetermined sequences or prescribed information to be taught at a given moment.

Curriculum webs can be a valuable resource in your efforts to build a Peaceable Classroom.* They provide *a procedure for quickly recording and organizing a great deal of information about a classroom in a visually clear and easy-to-read fashion.* They can help you:

- brainstorm ideas for activities around a subject area, topic, or issue that has come up in the classroom;

- see interconnections among various aspects of your curriculum and classroom;

- achieve a balance between allowing children input into the curriculum and guiding and directing their learning yourself;

- develop curriculum collaboratively with other adults such that everyone's ideas can be readily incorporated and discussed;

- keep track of the curriculum you have followed for a specific topic, issue, or skill throughout the year;

- communicate effectively with parents and other school personnel about activities in your classroom.

---

* For more detailed discussions of curriculum webs in the curriculum development process see D. Levin, "Weaving Curriculum Webs: Planning, Guiding, and Recording Curriculum Activities in the Day Care Classroom," *Day Care and Early Education* 13, no. 4 (Summer 1986): 16-19; and S. Workman and M. Anziano, "Curriculum Webs: Weaving Connections From Children to Teachers," *Young Children* 48, no. 2 (January 1993): 4-9.

A CURRICULUM WEB PLANNING MEDICAL PLAY

Figure 15 is the kind of web the teacher in Chapter 5 used to plan the hospital play in her classroom's dramatic play area. It includes her initial ideas about where to start the curriculum. Once the hospital project began, she circled the items that were covered and added to and modified the web, based on the children's responses and input.

FIGURE 15
MEDICAL PLAY CURRICULUM WEB

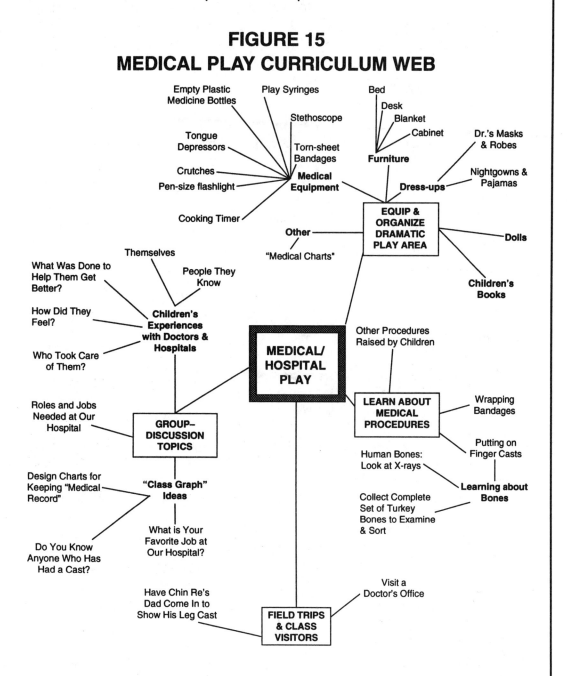

A CURRICULUM WEB DOCUMENTING THE USE OF A CLASS HISTORY CHART

Figure 16 is the curriculum web used by the teacher who did the class history chart described in Chapter 9. She developed it several months into the school year to record activities to date and the kinds of learning they had promoted. She also used it to evaluate how well she was incorporating literacy, numeracy, and social studies into her curriculum; to help her discuss her curriculum with parents on a special parents' night; and to help other teachers in her school start thinking about using class history charts in their own classrooms.

FIGURE 16
CLASS HISTORY CHART CURRICULUM WEB

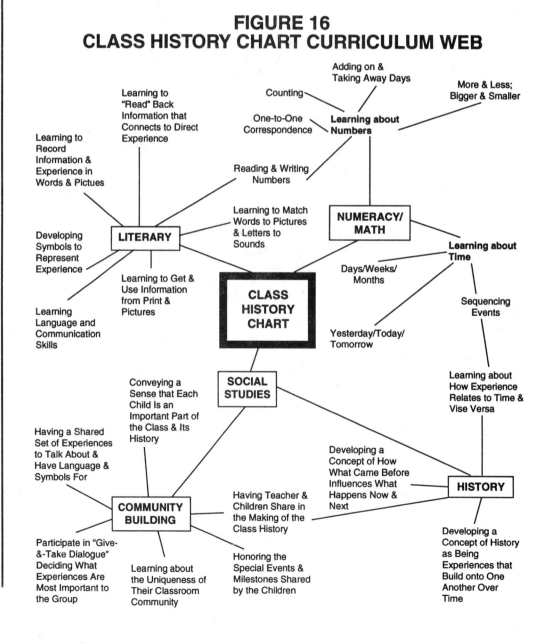

EXAMPLES OF OTHER WAYS TO USE CURRICULUM WEBS

Curriculum webs can also be used to:

- *keep track of and plan for individual children.* Include such information as what the child has done, particular needs, and special interests. Then you can use another color pen to add on new ideas for what you can try next with that child. Webs like this can also be helpful for planning what to discuss about a child at parent conferences. And they can help teaching teams to coordinate their efforts with individual children. This is especially so in inclusive classrooms where special needs children are enrolled.

- *brainstorm ways to deal with a problem in the classroom.* For instance, the teacher who at a class meeting developed the "Helper Chart" (described in Chapters 4 and 9) might have first made a quick web, brainstorming possible approaches for dealing with the children's seeming dependence on her. She might then have decided that addressing the problem at a meeting was the most likely to accomplish her goals of making the children less dependent on her and more interdependent with each other.

Implications for Practice:

If you have never used curriculum webs, or have never used them in the open-ended, multiple-purpose ways described here, there are a few things that might help you in your efforts:

- ☐ **There is no one right set of information for a given web**. The categories you use and information you include should depend on your purposes for making the web.

- ☐ **There is not one right place to put each item included in the web**. In fact, most entries could appropriately go in more than one place (and maybe they should).

- ☐ **The first web you try is likely to be the hardest**. For many of us it's hard to stop worrying about getting the web right and, instead, use it to brainstorm in a way that helps us quickly collect and organize a lot of useful ideas and information.

Chapter 14

ADDITIONAL READINGS AND RESOURCES

American Psychological Association. *Violence and Youth: Psychology's Response. Vol. I: Summary Report of the APA Commission on Violence and Youth.* Washington, DC: American Psychology Association, 1993.

Balaban, N. *Starting School: From Separation to Independence.* New York: Teachers College Press, 1985.

Bredekamp, S. ed. *Developmentally Appropriate Practice in Early Childhood Programs Serving Children from Birth through Age 8. Expanded Ed.* Washington, DC: National Association for the Education of Young Children, 1987.

Bredekamp, S. and T. Rosegrant, eds. *Reaching potentials: Appropriate Curriculum and Assessment for Young Children.* Washington, DC: National Association for the Education of Young Children, 1992.

Carlsson-Paige, N., and Levin, D.E. *Helping Young Children Understand Peace, War, and the Nuclear Threat.* Washington, DC: National Association for the Education of Young Children, 1985.

_____. "The Butter Battle Book: Uses and Abuses with Young Children." *Young Children* 41, no. 3 (March 1986): 37-42.

_____. *The War Play Dilemma: Balancing Needs and Values in the Early Childhood Classroom.* New York: Teachers College Press, 1987.

_____. *Who's Calling the Shots?: How to Respond Effectively to Children's Fascination with War Play and War Toys.* Philadelphia: New Society Publishers, 1990.

_____. "Children and the Crisis in the Persian Gulf." *Family Day Caring* (March/April 1991): 4-5.

_____. "The Subversion of Healthy Development and Play: Teachers' Reactions to the Teenage Mutant Ninja Turtles." *Day Care and Early Education* 19, no. 2 (Winter 1991): 14-20.

_____. "Moving Children from Time-out to Win/Win." *Child Care Information Exchange* 84 (March-April 1992): 38-42.

_____. "When Push Comes to Shove—Reconsidering Children's Conflicts." *Child Care Information Exchange* 84 (March-April 1992): 34-37.

_____. "Making Peace in Violent Times: A Constructivist Approach to Conflict Resolution." *Young Children* 48, no. 1 (November 1992): 4-13.

Children's Defense Fund. *The State of America's Children*. Washington, DC: Children's Defense Fund, 1992.

Committee for Children. *Second Step: A Violence-Prevention Curriculum. Preschool-Kindergarten*. Seattle: Committee for Children, 1991.

Craig, S. "The Educational Needs of Children Living with Violence." *Phi Delta Kappan*. 74, no. 1 (September 1992): 67-71.

Crary, E. *Kids Can Cooperate: A Practical Guide to Teaching Problem Solving*. Seattle: Parenting Press, 1984.

Curry, N.E. and C.N. Johnson. *Beyond Self-esteem: Developing a Genuine Sense of Human Value*. Washington, DC: National Association for Educators of Young Children, 1990.

Danielson, J.B. "Controversial Issues and Young Children: Kindergartners Try to Understand Chernobyl." In *Promising Practices in Teaching Social Responsibility*, edited by S. Berman and P. LaFarge. Albany, NY: State University of New York Press, 1993.

Davidson, J. "Literature as the Catalyst for Dramatic Play," In *Dramatic Play and Emergent Literacy: Natural Partners*. New York: Delmar, in press.

Derman-Sparks, L., and the A.B.C. Task Force. *The Anti-Bias Curriculum: Tools for Empowering Young Children*. Washington, DC: National Association for the Education of Young Children, 1989.

Derman-Sparks, L., and K. Taus. "We're Friends: Understanding Diversity Through Storytelling." *Pre K Today* 4, no. 3 (November-December 1989): 40-46, 60.

DeVries, R. and B. Zan. *Moral Classrooms, Moral Children: Creating a Constructivist Atmosphere in Early Education.* New York: Teachers College Press, 1994.

Edwards, C. *Promoting Social and Moral Development in Young Children: Creative Approaches for the Classroom.* New York: Teachers College Press, 1986.

Edwards, C.. "Creating Safe Places for Conflict to Happen" *Child Care Information Exchange* 84 (March-April 1992): 43-45.

Edwards, C., L. Gandini, and G. Forman, eds. *The Hundred Languages of Children: The Reggio Emilia Approach to Early Childhood Education.* Norwood, NJ: Ablex, 1993.

Eth, S., and R. Pynoos. *Post-traumatic Stress Disorder in Children.* Washington, DC: American Psychiatric Press, 1985.

Fisher, R., and W. Ury. *Getting to Yes: Negotiating Agreement without Giving In.* New York: Penguin Books, 1981.

Foyle, H., L. Lyman, and S. Alexander Thies. *Cooperative Learning in the Early Childhood Classroom.* Washington, DC: National Education Association of the US, 1991.

Garbarino, J., et al. *Children in Danger: Coping with the Consequences of Community Violence.* San Francisco: Jossey-Bass, 1992.

Greenberg, P. "Ideas That Work with Young Children. How to Institute Some Simple Democratic Practices Pertaining to Respect, Rights, Roots, and Responsibilities in Any Classroom (Without Losing Your Control)." *Young Children* 47, no. 5 (July 1992): 10-17.

Groves, B., et al. "Silent Victims: Children Who Witness Violence." *Journal of the American Medical Association* 269, no. 2 (13 January 1993): 262-264.

Hendrick, J. "Where Does It All Begin? Teaching the Principles of Democracy in the Early Years." *Young Children* 47, no. 3 (March 1992): 51-53.

Hopkins, S., and J. Winters. *Discover the World: Empowering Children to Value Themselves, Others and the Earth.* Philadelphia: New Society Publishers, 1990.

Hesse, P. *The World is a Dangerous Place: Images of the Enemy on Children's Television.* Cambridge, MA: Center for Psychology and Social Change, 1989. Videotape.

Judson, S., ed. *A Manual on Nonviolence and Children.* Philadelphia: New Society Publishers, 1984.

Kamii, C., and R. DeVries. *Group Games in Early Education: Implications of Piaget's Theory.* Washington, DC: National Association for the Education of Young Children, 1980.

Katz, L., and S. Chard. *Engaging Children's Minds: The Project Approach.* Norwood, NJ: Ablex, 1989.

Kohlberg, L. and T. Lickona. "Moral Discussion and the Class Meeting." In *Constructivist Early Education: Overview and Comparison with Other Programs,* edited by R. DeVries and L. Kohlberg. Washington, DC: National Association for the Education of Young Children, 1987.

Kohn, A. *No Contest: The Case against Competition.* Boston: Houghton Mifflin, 1986.

————· *Punished by Rewards: The Trouble with Gold Stars, Incentive Plans, Praise and Other Bribes.* Boston: Houghton Mifflin, 1993.

Kreidler, W.J. *Creative Conflict Resolution: More than 200 Activities for Keeping Peace in the Classroom.* Glencoe, IL: Scott, Foresman, 1984.

————· *Elementary Perspectives: Teaching Concepts of Peace and Conflict.* Cambridge, MA: Educators for Social Responsibility, 1990.

Levin, D. "Weaving Curriculum Webs: Planning, Guiding, and Recording Curriculum Activities in the Day Care Classroom." *Day Care and Early Education* 13, no. 4 (Summer 1986): 16-19.

Levin, D., and N. Carlsson-Paige. "Television for (Not against) Children: Developmentally Appropriate Programming." *Young Children,* in press.

Levin, D., and A. Klein. "What Did You Do in School Today: Using the School Environment to Foster Communication between Children and Parents." *Day Care and Early Education* 15, no. 3 (Spring 1988): 6-10.

Luvmour, S., and J. Luvmour. *Everyone Wins! Cooperative Games and Activities.* Philadelphia: New Society Publishers, 1990.

Mallory, B.L., and R.S. New. *Diversity and Developmentally Appropriate Practice: Challenges for Early Childhood Education.* New York: Teachers College Press, 1994.

McCracken, J.B. *Valuing Diversity: The Primary Years.* Washington, DC: National Association for the Education of Young Children, 1993.

McGinnis, E. and A. Goldstein. *Skill Streaming in Early Childhood: Teaching Prosocial Skills to the Preschool and Kindergarten Child.* Champaign, IL: Research Press, 1990.

McGinnis, K. and B. Oehlberg. *Starting Out Right: Nurturing Young Children As Peacemakers.* Oak Park, IL: Meyer-Stone Books, 1988.

Miedzian, M. *Boys Will Be Boys: Breaking the Link Between Masculinity and Violence.* New York: Doubleday, 1991.

Morrow, G. *The Compassionate School: A Practical Guide to Educating Abused and Traumatized Children.* Englewood Cliffs, NJ: Prentice Hall, 1987.

National Association for the Education of Young Children. "NAEYC Position Statement on Media Violence in Children's Lives. Adopted April 1990." *Young Children* 45, no. 5 (July 1990): 18-21.

————· "NAEYC Position Statement on Violence in the Lives of Children. Adopted July 1993." *Young Children* 48, no. 6 (September 1993): 80-84.

Neugebauer, B., ed. *Alike and Different: Exploring Our Humanity with Young Children.* Washington, DC: National Association for the Education of Young Children, 1992.

Parry, A. "Children Surviving in a Violent World–Choosing Non-Violence." *Young Children* 48, no. 6 (September 1993): 13-15.

Ramsey, P. G. *Teaching and Learning in a Diverse World.* New York: Teachers College Press, 1987.

———· *Making Friends in School: Promoting Peer Relationships in Early Childhood.* New York: Teachers College Press, 1991.

Reynolds, E. *Guiding Young Children: A Child-centered Approach.* Mountain View, CA: Mayfield Publishing, 1990.

Scheff, D. *Game Over: How Nintendo Zapped an American Industry, Captured Your Dollars and Enslaved Your Children.* New York: Random House, 1993.

Smith, C.A. *Promoting the Social Development of Young Children: Strategies and Activities.* Palo Alto, CA: Mayfield Publishing, 1982.

Thomson, B.J. *Words Can Hurt You: Beginning a Program of Anti-bias Education.* Menlo Park, CA: Addison Wesley, 1993.

Tuchscherer, P. *TV Interactive Toys: The New High Tech Threat to Children.* Bend, OR: Pinaroo Publishing, 1988.

Wallach, L. "Helping Young Children Cope with Violence." *Young Children* 48, no. 4 (May 1993): 4-11.

Wassermann, S. *Serious Players in the Primary Classrooms: Empowering Children through Active Learning Experiences.* New York: Teachers College Press, 1992.

Watson, M., et al. "The Child Development Project: Combining Traditional and Developmental Approaches to Values Education." In *Moral Development and Character Education: A Dialogue*, edited by L. Nucci. Berkeley, CA: McCutchan, 1989.

Watson, M., C. Hildebrandt, and D. Solomon. "Cooperative Learning as a Means of Promoting Prosocial Development Among Kindergarten and Early Primary-grade Children." *International Journal of Social Education* 3, no. 2 (Autumn 1988): 34-47.

Wichert, S. *Keeping the Peace: Practicing Cooperation and Conflict Resolution with Preschoolers.* Philadelphia: New Society Publishers, 1989.

Workman, S., and M. Anziano, "Curriculum Webs: Weaving Connections from Children to Teachers," *Young Children* 48, no. 2 (January 1993): 4-9.

Zero to Three. *Can They Hope to Feel Safe Again? Impact of Community Violence on Infants, Toddlers, Their Parents and Practitioners.* Arlington, VA: National Center for Clinical Infant Programs, 1992.

Appendix A

- Violence as a Product of Injustice
  — CEASE's (Concerned Educators
  Allied for a Safe Environment)
  Statement on Violence

- NAEYC (National Association for the
  Education of Young Children) Position
  Statement on Violence in the Lives
  of Children

- NAEYC Position Statement on
  Media Violence in Children's Lives

The following statement was drawn up at CEASE's retreat in June 1993 and worked on by participants from California, Delaware, Pennsylvania, New York and Massachusetts. Please reproduce and distribute it where you can. We welcome your comments and hope that discussion around the issues it raises will prove useful as we work towards a more peaceful and just society.

Violence as a Product of Injustice
CEASE's Statement on Violence

Fundamental to the advocacy work of CEASE is the belief that our goal, the full and equal valuing of every child, depends upon the principles of peace and justice and the development of social structures which represent, support and ensure these values. The understanding of the violence of our society belongs in this context. Violence is rooted in structured inequality. It is integral to our history, intrinsic to the militarism of our foreign policy and instrumental in the repression of minorities and dissent. Violence with its many forms is a resource of the powerful to maintain control.

Inequality is structured by the institutions and values which empower some groups and disempower others: rich over poor, men over women, white over color, heterosexual over gay/lesbian, adults over children. Power determines the unequal distribution of resources for basic human needs, health care, housing and quality education. Banks do not invest in communities of the less powerful. TV and movies carry few and often distorted images of the powerless. The court system provides limited protection and redress to the victims of violence who are less powerful.

The violence which protects these structured inequalities from challenge is disguised, rationalized, even glorified. The violence which erupts as a reaction to unbearable conditions of deprivation, from cynicism or marginalization is often described as without cause, or treated as random acts of disturbed individuals. TV plays a role in this definition process. During a military bombing raid, chiefs of staff and news coverage encourages the public to accept and even celebrate the killing. During the L.A. "riots," the coverage focussed on the wanton, even whimsical violence, and not on the issue of injustice. Children's daily dose of TV includes numerous acts of violence presented as heroism, and accustoms them to social practices of domination and control.

Our educational system, based on ranking children, and competition, reflects and reinforces the inequities of society. Wealthy school districts have greater resources and materials than schools in poor neighborhoods. Within schools, children are sorted and divided in ways which too often mirror the ranking of the society. Girls who start off excelling, learn to fail in order to "fit in." Children of color are retained and put in special education classes at far higher rates than white children, often dropping out from schools which do not listen to or value them as people.

Early childhood educators concerned about the violence of our society need to work for government policies which reduce inequities and promote justice. Policies which:
- **support** and extend resources for basic human needs, economic security, health care, housing and education.
- **oppose** militarism and economic coercion as the basis of U.S. foreign policy.

- **endorse** human rights ordinances which protect people from discrimination on the basis of gender, race, disability or sexual orientation.
- **advocate** for the regulation of violence in children's television and oppose the practice of marketing toys of violence or sexism.

Early childhood educators, as professionals with a special responsibility to our field, need to foster educational practices which:
- **strengthen** the democratic classroom model, the inclusion of children in the classroom governance.
- **commit** to a curriculum of multicultural awareness and anti-bias.
- **encourage** the training of children in conflict resolution and mediation strategies which empower children to be their own advocates and learn a repertoire of skills for resolving their conflicts nonviolently;
- **emphasize** community, connectedness and cooperation as fundamental classroom and school system values.
- **reject** punishment and "time out" which isolate children without helping them to find solutions to their problems.
- **develop** multiple patterns of partnership with parents, affirming the fundamental significance of families and family diversity in the positive development of children.
- **recognize** that a significant and sometimes overlooked cause of violent behavior in children derives from their sense of justice; that aggression and defiance may be the child's effort to redress insults to self-esteem and perceived unfairness. Children's sense of justice should be respected at the same time as they are given acceptable ways to achieve justice.
- **promote** peace and justice education as the core curriculum. This means rejecting materials which accept dominance, and developing materials which examine social and political issues in developmentally appropriate ways. This also means reexamining the history curriculum, the legacy of Columbus and genocide, of slavery and western "expansion."
- **review** teacher education to reconsider the ways issues of inequity, competition, and discrimination are taught and modeled.

Early childhood educators know all too well the devastating effects of violence on children. This knowledge impels us to understand and help reduce the injustice and inequities which are the overwhelmingly significant causes of violence: The goal for our children and ourselves is to create a society where the ideals of peace, justice and democracy may be ever more fully realized. ◇

CEASE
17 Gerry Street
Cambridge, Massachusetts 02138

NAEYC Position Statement on
Violence in the Lives of Children

Adopted July 1993

The problem of violence

Tragically, every day children in America witness violent acts or are victims of abuse, neglect, or personal assault in their homes or communities. Marian Wright Edelman (1993) states, "[We] Adults have failed dismally in our most basic responsibility—to protect our society's children from violence," as the following facts and statistics reveal:

• The United States is now the most violent country in the industrialized world, leading the world in homicides, rapes, and assaults (Dodd, 1993; Weiner, 1991).

• An estimated 2.7 million children were reported to child protection agencies in 1991 as victims of neglect, physical abuse, sexual abuse, or emotional maltreatment; nationwide the number of children reported abused or neglected has tripled since 1980 (Children's Defense Fund, 1992).

• Gun-related violence takes the life of an American child at least every three hours and the lives of at least 25 children—the equivalent of a classroomful—every three days. In 1990 alone guns were used to kill 222 children under the age of 10 and 6,795 young people under the age of 25. Another 30 children are injured every day by guns (Edelman, 1993). Every day 100,000 children carry guns to school.

• In one Chicago public housing project all of the children had witnessed a shooting by the age of five

(Dodd, 1993). A child growing up in Chicago is 15 times as likely to be murdered as is a child growing up in Northern Ireland (Garbarino, 1992).

• By age 18 the average child will have seen 26,000 killings on television (Tuchscherer, 1988). *TV Guide* reports that a violent incident is shown on television, on the average, every six minutes (Edelman, 1993). The number of violent acts depicted on television has tripled since deregulation of the industry.

• In a national survey 91% of the responding teachers reported increased violence among children in their classrooms as a result of cross-media marketing of violent cartoons, toys, videos, and other licensed products (Carlsson-Paige & Levin, 1991).

• In a recent survey of New Orleans fifth graders more than half reported they had been victims of some type of violence; 70% had witnessed weapons being used (Zero to Three, 1992).

The escalating rate of violence in many American cities means that large numbers of children are growing up in conditions that have been described as "inner-city war zones" (Garbarino, Dubrow, Kostelny, & Pardo, 1992). But the problem of violence is not restricted to any one community or group. All children today are affected by the violence that pervades our society. As a result, the healthy development of many of our nation's children is in serious jeopardy.

The causes and effects of violent behavior in society are complex and interrelated; much violence results from social injustice prevalent in our society. Among the significant contributors are poverty, racism, unemployment, substance abuse, proliferation of guns, inadequate or abusive parenting practices, real-life adult models of violent problem-solving behavior, and frequent exposure to violence through the media. Today every fifth child lives in poverty; among children under the age of six the percentage is 25% (Children's Defense Fund, 1992). Basic services to low-income families have been drastically reduced in the last decade as federal funding has been cut. As social programs have disappeared and the economy has worsened, violence in homes, schools, and communities has increased. The proliferation of handguns has contributed greatly to the increase in violent assaults and homicides experienced by children (Garbarino, 1992).

The culture of violence is mirrored in and influenced by the media. As a result of the deregulation of the broadcasting industry, children's television and related toys have become more violent (Carlsson-Paige & Levin, 1990). Research is clear that the media, particularly television and films, contribute to the problem of violence in America (Slabey, 1992; Huesmann & Miller, in press). Research demonstrates that children who are frequent viewers of violence on television are less likely to show empathy toward the pain and suffering of others and more likely to behave aggressively.

Violence touches the life of every child in this country, some more directly than others. A continuum of exposure to violence exists that extends from exposure through the media to being a direct witness, being a victim, and, for too many children, becoming a perpetrator. There are many points along the way in this continuum that include frequent viewing of media violence and the commercial linkup of toys that promote violent behavior (for example, a popular line of male dolls now includes drug dealers), secondhand reports of acts of violence, warnings and admonitions by parents about personal safety, witnessing actual acts of violence to strangers or family members, witnessing or experiencing domestic violence, harming or killing someone else, being wounded or killed oneself. Recognizing the existence of this continuum of exposure to violence makes it evident that no child in America is exempt from some exposure. As U.S. Senator Christopher Dodd points out, "Violence is America's problem; from affluent suburbs to inner-city streets, violence knows no social, economic, racial, or geographic boundaries."

This country has committed itself to a national goal—by the year 2000: **All** children will start school ready to learn. Achieving this goal will be impossible unless the country also simultaneously breaks the cycle of violence that grips so many children and families. Children need to be safe and secure at home to develop a positive sense of self necessary to their growing into healthy, productive, caring adults; children need to be safe in their communities to be able to explore and develop relationships with other people; and children need to be safe at school in order to successfully learn.

The effects of violence on children

What is this tragedy doing to our children? A fundamental need of children is to feel safe; if children do not feel safe, they run the risk of becoming traumatized as victims or eventually becoming perpetrators themselves. Experts describe the impact of violence on many children as *post-traumatic stress disorder* (Garbarino et al., 1992) American children show symptoms similar to those first associated with some Vietnam veterans and children living in war-torn countries: sleep disturbances, inability to concentrate, flashbacks, images of terror, and nightmares.

The younger the child the greater is the threat of exposure to violence to healthy development. Individuals who experienced an initial trauma before the age of 11 were three times more likely to develop psychiatric symptoms than those who experienced their first trauma as teens (Davidson & Smith, 1990, quoted in Garbarino et al., 1992, p. 70). Chronic exposure to violence can have serious developmental consequences for children including psychological disorders, grief and loss reactions, impaired intellectual development and school problems, truncated moral development, pathological adaptation to violence, and identification with the aggressor (Craig, 1992; Garbarino et al., 1992). Not surprisingly, children exposed to violence have difficulty focusing on school work or engaging in any of the other playful activities that should be treasured experiences of childhood.

It is estimated that up to 80% of all children exposed to powerful stressors do not sustain developmental damage (Rutter, 1979; Werner, 1990). Research indicates that certain factors contribute to the resilience of these children. A child's individual characteristics and early life experiences, as well as protective factors in the child's physical and social environment, contribute to resilience. A number of protective factors in the environment are associated with resilience: a stable, emotional relationship with at least one parent or other significant adult; an open, supportive educational climate and parental model of behavior that encourage constructive coping with problems; and social support from persons outside the family. The most important buffer is a supportive relationship with parents. Most children are able to cope with dangerous environments and maintain resilience as long as their parents are not stressed beyond their capacity to cope (Garbarino et al., 1992). Schools and child care programs can be vitally important support systems by strengthening children's resilience and providing resources for parents so that they can serve as psychological buffers to protect their children.

What can be done?

The National Association for the Education of Young Children (NAEYC), the nation's largest professional organization of early childhood educators, is committed to actions that address two major goals:

1. To decrease the extent of violence in all forms in children's lives by advocating for public policies and actions at the national level; and

2. To enhance the ability of educators to help children cope with violence, and promote children's resilience, and assist families by improving professional practice in early childhood programs.

1—Advocate for public policies and actions

Many of the negative outcomes described above can be prevented if we are willing to take action on many fronts. First, the nation must begin focusing energy and resources on prevention rather than only supporting more criminal justice strategies that come after the fact and have not proven to be effective deterrents (Prothrow-Stith, 1993).

Every sector of our society must assume some responsibility for the problem. The challenge is to develop policies that reduce the number of risk factors for all children but especially for children from low-income families. Policies should target the greatest number of resources toward children in the preschool and elementary years when children are most vulnerable to developmental damage as a result of exposure to violence.

Several important steps are necessary for this nation to prevent violence in the lives of children:

• **Generate public outrage.** We believe that a necessary first step is to generate a sense of public outrage that motivates actions that will eliminate violence in the lives of children, families, and communities. Too many Americans believe that violence is something that happens to other people or only in some places; as a result, increasing violence in our nation has been met with surprising apathy. Only when violence hits close to home do citizens become sufficiently mobilized to take action, often too late. Many adults are so overwhelmed by constant exposure to violence in the media, on the streets, and in the world that they become hopeless, desensitized, or disempowered to act.

• **Allocate resources to prevention of violence.** In 1980 there were 500,000 inmates in jails and prisons in the United States; in 1990 there were 1,000,000. The previous decade of getting tough on crime saw a 12% increase in violent crime (Prothrow-Stith, 1993). It is obvious that criminal-justice efforts alone will not slow the rate of violence. Such efforts must be

combined with equal or greater resources allocated to proven strategies that prevent violence, starting with programs targeted to support families with young children.

• **Generate commitment to the right of every child to a safe, non-violent, and nurturing society.** Our nation must commit itself to changing the conditions in which children live, reducing the number of risk factors that children experience, and enhancing social and psychological resources. Policies must support the provision of jobs that pay adequate wages, affordable housing, adequate health care, strong supportive families, high-quality early childhood and school-age programs, and safe neighborhoods.

• **Revitalize neighborhoods through ensuring peacekeeping and targeting the delivery of human services, such as job training, health care, early childhood education programs, and parent education.** Although violence is a problem that affects our entire nation, violence in inner cities requires targeted assistance to save the children and break the cycle of violence. Resources must become available for programs that address violence prevention through legislation, such as the Child and Family Services and Law Enforcement Partnership Act. Increased funding is needed for family support programs that equip parents with coping skills while also developing positive parenting behaviors. Resources are also needed to assist children who are victims of violence.

• **Support efforts to limit the availability of firearms and other weapons, especially their access to children.** If firearms kept people safe, the United States would be the safest country in the world because so many firearms are readily available. In the state of Texas, for instance, there are four guns available for every citizen. Instead, we are the most violent industrial-

ized country in the world. According to the Center To Prevent Handgun Violence, in 1990 handguns were used to kill 87 people in Japan, 68 in Canada, 22 in Great Britain, 10 in Australia, and 10,567 in the United States. If we are ever to achieve safe schools and communities for our children, this nation must limit the availability of firearms and other weapons. Large numbers of children are "accidentally" injured or killed by guns; these injuries or deaths are preventable by limiting children's access to firearms.

• **Regulate children's television programming to limit media exposure to violence and restrict practices that market violence through the linkup of media, toys, and licensed products.** Since deregulation in the early 1980s, children's exposure to violence through the media has gone unchecked. At the same time longitudinal data have become available that clearly link media viewing of violent acts with increased violent behaviors. Presumably broadcasters would act responsibly to limit exposure to violence without the constraint of regulation, but this has not been the case. The Federal Communications Commission should regulate the amount of violence on children's television and, as a condition for license renewal, review television station's efforts and accomplishments in helping serve the information and educational needs of children regarding violence and how to prevent it. The powerful linkup of commercial products with programs depicting violence has well-documented negative effects on children's development (Carlsson-Paige & Levin, 1990). Regulation is also needed to control practices that market violence to children through the linkup of media, toys, and licensed products. (See NAEYC Position Statement on Media Violence in Children's Lives,

1990). Violence in film and film previews is increasing, and previews are shown even during family films and during children's TV.

• **Prohibit corporal punishment in schools and all other programs for children.** Numerous states continue to permit corporal punishment in schools or child care programs. Some states that prohibit corporal punishment in standards for licensing child care programs allow exemptions for certain types of programs or under certain conditions. The institutional use of corporal punishment in such situations teaches children that physical solutions to problems are acceptable for adults and that aggression is an appropriate way to control the behavior of other people. The institutional use of corporal punishment should never be condoned.

2—Commit the early childhood profession to helping children cope with violence in their lives and promoting their resilience through partnerships with parents; early childhood programs and curriculum; and professional preparation, development, and support.

As do all sectors of society, the early childhood profession has an important role to play in breaking the cycle of violence in the lives of children. Specific recommendations for action follow in each of three areas.

Partnerships with parents. Early childhood professionals must help families deal with stress and enhance their ability to help children cope with violence. The needs of families also range along a continuum. Popular culture socializes children into violent behavior so effectively that society is actually undermining parents' ability to protect their own children. Some parents are victims of violence themselves. Many are so stressed by community conditions that they are unable to serve as the buffer of emotional protection that children need. Finally, some parents are perpetrators of violence themselves, and in some cases their children are their own victims. NAEYC is committed to actions that support families, such as the following:

• Increase awareness on the part of families about the profound effects of violence on children.

• Support the critical role that parents play in promoting the development of prosocial behavior.

• Collaborate with parents to bring about changes needed in local communities to prevent violence.

• Support the importance of the parental role in the lives of children by providing education for parenthood, helping parents develop positive parenting skills, and supporting proven programs that prevent child abuse and neglect.

• Increase the ability of families to find and use community resources to support and protect children and families.

Early childhood programs and curriculum. We should not underestimate the important role that early childhood programs can play in supporting the healthy development of children and families. Although high-quality early childhood programs are *not* an inoculation against the destructive effects of violence, positive early school experiences and warm, nurturing relationships with teachers are known to be critical contributors to children's ability to cope with stress and trauma. To achieve this potential such programs must meet the highest possible professional standards, teachers must be well trained and compensated, and comprehensive support systems must be in place. NAEYC is committed to the following goals:

• Ensure that high-quality, developmentally appropriate early childhood programs are available to all children. Such programs comply with NAEYC's standards for accreditation (NAEYC, 1992) and developmentally appropriate practice (Bredekamp, 1987) and provide adequate salaries to ensure continuity of qualified staff.

• Ensure that all early childhood programs that serve children who are exposed to violence are able to provide comprehensive physical, social, and mental health services; and family involvement.

• Provide guidance to early childhood educators on how to create a sense of community in their classroom by infusing democratic processes and on the promotion of social competence into the total school environment and daily classroom life (for example, supportive warm-and-caring relationships with adults; an organized and predictable environment; and a developmental curriculum that fosters self-esteem and integrates therapeutic and healing strategies, such as play and art). (See Wallach, 1993.)

• Promote curriculum and teaching practices that address violence prevention; teach conflict resolution, cooperative learning, respect for diversity in all its forms; and promote positive cultural identity as a central part of the program (Carlsson-Paige & Levin, 1992).

• Support individualized, early intervention for children who are victims of violence and strengthen training for all personnel on violence counseling.

Professional preparation, development, and support. Studies have shown that positive school experiences are a major contributor to the resilience of children who are exposed to stress. Of special importance is a trusting relationship with a preschool or primary school teacher. Most teachers, however, have not been trained to help children cope with the effects of violence, nor have they learned how to teach children alternatives to violent behavior. In addition, schools in urban areas with high levels of poverty have the highest levels of violence but the fewest resources to combat them. Adults who care for victimized children over long periods of time are themselves in psychological peril. NAEYC is committed to the following actions:

• Provide teacher education programs that address the areas of child development theory and practice, root causes of violence in children's lives, the developmental consequences of stress and trauma, protective factors and resilience, the development of mental health skills, emotional availability and the role of affect in helping relationships, advocacy skills to help eliminate causes of violence, and the use of community and professional resources.

• Revise teacher certification standards to require violence-prevention training and the teaching of alternatives to violence.

• Create in-service teacher education programs on helping children cope with violence in their lives, with special emphasis on the therapeutic strategies of children's play and art.

• Develop ongoing consultation services for teachers, especially those who work with children in violent communities, to support teachers' mental health, address their fears and trauma, and provide assistance as they work with children who have multiple needs.

Conclusion

The violence that plagues our nation has many sources, and its elimination will require systematic attention at many levels. Most importantly, the citizens of our na-

tion must become outraged at the victimization of its children and must turn this outrage into positive action and increased resources toward preventing violence in the lives of children. All adults must assume the responsibility for keeping children safe. Our society cannot afford the devastating effects of failing to protect its children. Each of us individually must commit ourselves to the actions that are most appropriate for our own sphere of influence. The early childhood profession individually and collectively must work to influence public commitment, action, and policy and collaborate with other organizations to reduce the causes of violence. The early childhood profession must also address issues of violence in children's lives through partnerships with parents and other professionals; early childhood programs and curriculum; and professional preparation, development, and support.

References

Bredekamp, S. (Ed.). (1987). *Developmentally appropriate practice in early childhood programs serving children from birth through age 8* (exp. ed.). Washington, DC: NAEYC.

Carlsson-Paige, N., & Levin, D.E. (1990). Who's calling the shots? How to respond effectively to children's fascination with war play and war toys. Philadelphia: New Society Publishers.

Carlsson-Paige, N., & Levin, D.E. (1991). The subversion of healthy development and play. *Day Care and Early Education, 19*(2), 14–20.

Carlsson-Paige, N., & Levin, D.E. (1992). Making peace in violent times: A constructivist approach to conflict resolution. *Young Children, 48*(1), 4–13.

Children's Defense Fund (CDF). (1992). *The state of America's children, 1992*. Washington, DC: Author.

Craig, S. (1992). The educational needs of children living with violence. *Phi Delta Kappan, 74*(1), 67–71.

Dodd, C. (1993). Testimony prepared for the Joint Senate-House Hearing on Keeping Every Child Safe: Curbing the Epidemic of Violence. 103rd Cong., 1st sess., March 10.

Edelman, M.W. (1993). Testimony prepared for the Joint Senate-House Hearing on Keeping Every Child Safe: Curbing the Epidemic of Violence. 103rd Cong., 1st sess., March 10.

Garbarino, J. (1992, November). *Helping children cope with the effects of community violence.* Paper presented at the Annual Conference of the National Association for the Education of Young Children, New Orleans, LA.

Garbarino, J., Dubrow, N., Kostelny, K., & Pardo, C. (1992). *Children in danger: Coping with the effects of community violence.* San Francisco, CA: Jossey-Bass.

Huesmann, L.R., & Miller, L. (in press). Long-term effects of repeated exposure to media violence in childhood. In L.R. Huesmann (Ed.), *Aggressive behavior: Current perspectives.* NY: Plenum.

National Association for the Education of Young Children (NAEYC). (1990). NAEYC position statement on media violence in children's lives. *Young Children, 45*(5), 18-21.

National Association for the Education of Young Children (NAEYC). (1992). *Accreditation criteria & procedures of the National Academy of Early Childhood Programs* (rev. ed.). Washington, DC: Author.

Prothrow-Stith, D. (1993). Testimony prepared for the Joint Senate-House Hearing on Keeping Every Child Safe: Curbing the Epidemic of Violence. 103rd Cong., 1st sess., March 10.

Rutter, M. (1979). Protective factors in children's responses to stress and disadvantage. In M.W. Kent & J.E. Rolf (Eds.), *Primary prevention of psychopathology: Social competence in children* Vol. 3 (pp. 49–74). Hanover, NH: University Press of New England.

Slabey, R.G. (1992). The prevention of youth violence. Testimony prepareed for the U.S. Senate Committee on Governmental Affairs. 102nd Cong., 2ndsess., March 31.

Tuchscherer, P. (1988). *TV interactive toys: The new high tech threat to children.* Bend, OR: Pinnaroo Publishing.

Wallach, L. (1993). Helping children cope with violence. *Young Children, 48*(4), 4–11.

Weiner, T. (1991, March 13). Senate unit calls US most violent country on earth. The Boston Globe, p. 3.

Werner, E.E. (1990). Protective factors and individual resilience. In S.J. Meisels & J.P. Shonkoff (Eds.), Handbook of early childhood education (pp. 97–116). Cambridge, England: Cambridge University Press.

Zero to Three. (1992). *Can they hope to feel safe again? Impact of community violence on infants, toddlers, their parents and practitioners.* Arlington, VA: National Center for Clinical Infant Programs.

NAEYC Position Statement on Media Violence in Children's Lives

Adopted April 1990

During the past decade, America has witnessed an alarming increase in the incidence of violence in the lives of children. On a daily basis, children in America are victims of violence, as witnesses to violent acts in their homes or communities, or as victims of abuse, neglect, or personal assault. The causes of violent behavior in society are complex and interrelated. Among the significant contributors are poverty, racism, unemployment, illegal drugs, inadequate or abusive parenting practices, and real-life adult models of violent problem-solving behavior. NAEYC, the nation's largest organization of early childhood professionals, is deeply concerned about the destructive effect of violent living conditions and experiences on many of our nation's children.

At the same time that there has been an increase in the number of reported violent acts directed at children, there has been an increase in the amount and severity of violent acts observed by children through the media, including television, movies, computer games, and videotapes, and an increase in the manufacture and distribution of weapon-like toys and other products directly linked to violent programming. NAEYC believes the trend toward increased depiction of violence in the media jeopardizes the healthy development of significant numbers of our nation's children.

In response, NAEYC's Governing Board appointed a panel of experts to guide the development of initiatives and resources to assist teachers and parents in confronting the issue of violence in the lives of children. This position statement addresses one aspect of the problem—media violence—and is the first in a series of projects the Association plans to address this important issue. We have chosen to address the issue of media violence first because, of all the sources and manifestations of violence in children's lives, it is perhaps the most easily corrected. The media industry ought to serve the public interest and ought to be subject to government regulation.

Statement of the position

NAEYC condemns violent television programming, movies, videotapes, computer games, and other forms of media directed to children. NAEYC believes that it is the responsibility of adults and of public policy to protect children from unnecessary and potentially harmful exposure to violence through the media and to protect children from television content and advertising practices that exploit their special vulnerability (Huston, Watkins, & Kunkel, 1989). NAEYC believes that television and other media have the potential to be very effective educational tools for children. Research demonstrates that television viewing is a highly complex, cognitive activity, during which children are actively involved in learning (Anderson & Collins, 1988). Therefore, NAEYC supports efforts to use media constructively to expand children's knowledge and promote the development of positive social values. NAEYC also supports measures that can be taken by responsible adults to limit children's exposure to violence through the media. Such efforts include but are not limited to:

● legislation requiring reinstatement of guidelines for children's television by the Federal Communication Commission, including requirements for videotapes and elimination of television programs linked to toys

● legislation limiting advertising on children's programming, and standards for toys to ensure that they are not only physically safe, but also psychologically safe

● legislation enabling the development of voluntary television-industry standards to alleviate violence in programming, specifically exempting such efforts from anti-trust regulation

● promotion of more developmentally appropriate, educational programming that meets children's diverse needs for information, entertainment, aesthetic appreciation, positive role models, and knowledge about the world (Huston et al., 1989)

● development and dissemination of curriculum for teachers to improve children's critical viewing skills and to teach nonviolent strategies for resolving conflicts

● development of resources to assist parents in the constructive and educational use of media with their children

During early childhood, the foundation is laid for future social, emotional, cognitive, and physical development. During this formative period, young children are particularly vulnerable to negative influences. In most instances, children have no control over the environmental messages they receive. Up until age seven or eight, children have great difficulty distinguishing fantasy from reality and their ability to comprehend nuances of behavior, motivation, or moral complexity is limited. This special vulnerability of children necessitates increased vigilance to protect them from potentially negative influences. Parents are ultimately responsible for monitoring their children's viewing habits; however, parents cannot be omniscient and omnipresent in their children's lives. Parents need assistance in protecting their children from unhealthy exposure to violence. Therefore, limits must be placed on the content of programming directed at children. Restricting violence in children's programming should not be considered censorship, any more than is protecting children from exposure to pornography (Carlsson-Paige & Levin, 1990). Likewise, industry standards to limit violence in children's programming should be developed as action taken in the public interest.

Rationale

This position statement is based on research examining the amount of violence present in the media as well as the effect of exposure to violent programming on children's development. Data clearly indicate that violence in the media has increased since 1980 and continues to increase. In addition, there is clear evidence to support the negative impact of viewing violence on children's development.

How violent are the media for children?

The problem of violence in the media is not new, but has become much worse since the Federal Communication Commission's decision to deregulate children's commercial television in 1982. For example, air time for war cartoons jumped from 1½ hours per week in 1982 to 43 hours per week in 1986 (Carlsson-Paige & Levin, 1987; Tuscherer, 1988). Children's programs featured 18.6 violent acts per hour a decade ago and now have about 26.4 violent acts each hour (Gerbner, 1990). Adults need to recognize that the content of programming has changed, and as a result the potential for negative effects on children's development is greater. Next to the family, television and other media may be the most important sources of information for children, rivaling the school as a principal factor influencing their development.

How do violent media affect children's development?

Research consistently identifies three problems associated with heavy viewing of television violence: Children may become less sensitive to the pain and suffering of others; they may become more fearful of the world around them; and they may be more likely to behave in aggressive or harmful ways toward others (National Institute of Mental Health, 1982; Singer & Singer, 1984, 1986; Singer, Singer & Rapaczynski, 1984; Rule & Ferguson, 1986; Simon, 1989). Exposure to media violence leads children to see violence as a normal response to stress and as an acceptable means for resolving conflict.

Of great concern to early childhood educators is the negative effect of viewing violent programs on children's play. The importance of children's imaginative play to their cognitive and language development is well documented (Piaget, 1962, 1963; Johnson, Christie, & Yawkey, 1987). Research demonstrates that watching violent programs is related to less imaginative play and more imitative play in which the child simply mimics the aggressive acts observed on television (NIMH, 1982). In addition, many media productions that regularly depict violence also promote program-based toys, which encourage children to imitate and reproduce in their play the actual behaviors seen on television or in movies. In these situations, children's creative and imaginative play is undermined, thus robbing children of the benefits of play for their development (Carlsson-Paige & Levin, 1990). In their play, children imitate those characters reinforced for their aggressive behavior and rehearse the characters' scripts without creative or reflective thought. Children who repeatedly observe violent or aggressive problem-solving behavior in the media tend to rehearse what they see in their play and imitate those behaviors in real-life encounters (Huesmann, 1986; Rule & Ferguson, 1986; Eron & Huesmann, 1987). In short, children who are frequent viewers of media violence learn that aggression is a successful and acceptable way to achieve goals and solve problems; they are less likely to benefit from creative, imaginative play as the natural means to express feelings, overcome anger, and gain self-control.

Recommendations

What should policymakers and broadcasters do?

NAEYC supports the reinstitution of FCC standards establishing limits on violent depictions during hours children are likely to watch television. Standards would also control the degree to which violence is depicted so as to be perceived by children as a normal and acceptable response to problems, as equated with power, as leading to reward or glorification of the perpetrator. An additional strategy would be to develop a parental guidance rating system for network and cable television, videotapes, and computer games similar to that established for movies.

NAEYC further supports the reestablishment of industry standards to limit children's exposure to violence. The self-regulating code of the National Association of Broadcasters (1980) was a responsible position of the television industry toward young children. As an immediate action, laws prohibiting the adoption of such voluntary standards as violations of anti-trust regulation should be repealed.

Industry standards should also limit advertising during children's programming in recognition of children's inability to distinguish the advertising from programming content and to prevent acts of aggression or violence being separated from consequences by intervening commercials. Studies show that children up to eight years of age are less likely to "learn the lesson" of a program when ads intervene between an anti-social act and its consequences.

Finally, broadcasting standards should prohibit product-based programming and feature-length programs whose primary purpose is to sell toys, especially when those toys facilitate imitation of violent or aggressive acts seen on television. Children are unable to evaluate the quality and play value of such products depicted on television. Program-based advertising creates in children an insatiable desire for these single-use toys; children start to believe that they can't play without the specific props seen on television (Carlsson-Paige & Levin, 1990).

What can teachers do?

NAEYC believes that early childhood teachers have a responsibility to assist children in developing skills in nonviolent conflict resolution, to assist children to become critical viewers of all forms of media, and to encourage the constructive use of the media for instilling positive social values. Teachers need to be aware of what is currently being broadcast to children and to inform parents of the impact of violent media on children's development. Unfortunately, the effect of deregulation on the quality of children's television has made it necessary for teachers and parents to be more vigilant than they would have to be if the government and television industry acted more responsibly toward children.

Teachers can work with children when themes of television violence appear in their play to facilitate more appropriate problem solving and/or creative, imaginative play. Teachers should inform parents when negative or violent themes appear as a regular part of their children's play and support parents in their efforts to monitor children's viewing habits.

As professionals, early childhood educators should share their knowledge of child development and the effects of violent media viewing with legislators and sponsors of children's programming. It is the professional responsibility of early childhood educators to advocate for more developmentally and educationally appropriate programming for children. Teachers need to recognize that media are also a powerful teacher that can and should be used constructively with children. Contrary to popular belief, television viewing is not a passive activity; children are mentally active during television viewing (Anderson & Collins, 1988). The use of media as an educational tool should not be rejected because much of commercial television currently lacks educational value or promotes violence. Instead, early childhood professionals should advocate for policy that eliminates violence and improves the educational value of media, and should use media constructively in their work with children.

What can parents do?

The absence of governmental regulation of children's television has made parents' job more difficult, necessitating more parental monitoring of what children see on television. This unfortunate situation places additional, unnecessary pressure on parents. Even when industry standards are developed, NAEYC believes that parents are responsible for monitoring the quality and quantity of the media to which their children are exposed. Standards will make the job easier, however. In the meantime, parents can watch television and other media with their children and evaluate the shows together. Children do not interpret programs the same way adults do. Adults need to talk with children about what they observe through the media, to find out how children are interpreting what they see, and to help clarify misinterpretations. Parents can designate an approved list of media options for thier children and give children choices from among approved shows.

Parents need to be aware that much of what children watch on television is not specifically intended for children. It has been estimated that only 10% of children's viewing time is spent watching children's television; the other 90% is spent watching programs designed for adults (Van Dyck, 1983). Parents can assist children in finding alternatives to viewing adult television. In addition, parents can use videotapes of high-quality children's programming and public television when commercial alternatives are not available.

As consumers, parents should recognize and use their influence with sponsors of children's programs. The primary purpose of commercial television is not to entertain or to educate but to sell products. Parents can communicate with advertisers on programs that are valuable, as well as sponsors of programs that are violent. Parents can also help their children become educated consumers and involve them in writing complaints to broadcasters and companies that use violent images in an attempt to sell toys and other products. As taxpayers, parents can encourage their legislators to adopt policies to protect children from media violence.

Conclusion

The prevalence of violence in American society is a complex social problem that will not be easily solved. Violence in the media is only one manifestation of the larger society's fascination with violence. However, media violence is not just a reflection of a violent society, it is also a contributor. If our nation wishes to produce future generations of productive adults who reject violence as a means of problem solving, we must reassert the vital role of government in protecting its most vulnerable citizens and, together, work to make media part of the solution.

References

Anderson, D., & Collins, P. (1988). *The impact on children's education: Television's influence on cognitive development*. Washington, DC: U.S. Department of Education, Office of Educational Research and Improvement.

Carlsson-Paige, N., & Levin, D. (1987). *The war play dilemma: Balancing needs and values in the early childhood classroom*. New York: Teachers College Press, Columbia University.

Carlsson-Paige, N., & Levin, D. (1990). *Who's calling the shots? How to respond effectively to children's fascination with war play and war toys*. Santa Cruz, CA: New Society Publishers.

Eron, L., & Huesmann, L. (1987). Television as a source of maltreatment of children. *School Psychology Review, 16*, 195–202.

Gerbner, G., & Signorielli, N. (1990). *Violence profile 1967 through 1988–89: Enduring trends*. Philadelphia: University of Pennsylvania, Annenberg School of Communication.

Huesmann, L. (1986). Psychological processes promoting the relation between exposure to media violence and aggressive behavior by the viewer. *Journal of Social Issues, 42*, 125–140.

Huston, A., Watkins, B., & Kunkel, D. (1989). Public policy and children's television. *American Psychologist, 44*, 424–433.

Johnson, J., Christie, J., & Yawkey, T. (1987). *Play and early childhood development*. Glenview, IL: Scott, Foresman.

National Association of Broadcasters. (1980). *The television code* (21st ed.). New York: Author.

National Institute of Mental Health. (1982). *Television and behavior: Ten years of scientific progress for the eighties. Vol. 1: Summary Report*. Washington, DC: U.S. Government Printing Office.

Piaget, J. (1962). *Play, dreams, and imitation in children* (C. Gattegno & F. M. Hodgson, Trans.). New York: Norton. (Original work published 1951)

Piaget, J. (1963). *The origins of intelligence in children*. (M. Cook, Trans.). New York: Norton. (Original work published 1936)

Rule, B., & Ferguson, T. (1986). The effects of media violence on attitudes, emotions and cognitions. *Journal of Social Issues, 42*, 29–50.

Simon, P. (1989, August 21). Coming soon: An act that should reduce television violence. *Newsday*.

Singer, D., & Singer, J. (1984). TV violence: What's all the fuss about? *Television & Children, 7*(2), 30–41.

Singer, J. L., & Singer, D. G. (1986). Family experiences and television viewing as predictors of children's imagination, restlessness, and aggression. *Journal of Social Issues, 42*, 107–124.

Singer, J., Singer, D., & Rapaczynski, W. (1984). *Journal of Communicaton, 34*(2), 73–89.

Tuscherer, P. (1988). *TV interactive toys: The new high tech threat to children*. Bend, OR: Pinnaroo Publishing.

Van Dyck, N. B. (1983). Families and television. *Television & Children, 6*(3), 3–11.

Appendix B

The Mighty Morphin Power Rangers: A New Violent TV Show and Toy Line Enters the Popular Culture of Young Children

Just as this book was completed, the Mighty Morphin Power Rangers arrived on the scene in the form of a TV show, line of toys, and numerous other licensed products. The Power Rangers have seemingly become an overnight success. Called the "Cabbage Patch Dolls of the December 1993 holiday season," stores around the country have been unable to keep the toys stocked on the shelves. Teachers and parents have already begun to voice concern and ask for help.

Power Rangers add a new dimension to the problems created for children by violent cartoons and toy lines like the Teenage Mutant Ninja Turtles that are described in this book. The show mixes footage of the real actor Power Rangers (the good guys & gals) with footage of animated monsters (the bad guys) who regularly and brutally attack the Power Rangers. This dual technique thoroughly confuses most young children as they try to sort out fantasy from reality, good from bad, and violence from non-violence. In the words of one teacher, "After I watched the show, I understood why the children in my class are continually arguing over whether the Power Rangers are pretend or real." Such confusion further undermines children's ability to keep media violence separate from their real life behavior and ideas. And those children who are already having the hardest time with this are most at risk of being affected negatively.

Try to keep an eye out for how the Power Rangers are affecting the children in your classroom and use the guidelines in this book for trying to counteract the negative effects you see. This is one way you can work to avoid a situation from developing similar to when the Teenage Mutant Ninja Turtles arrived on the scene and caught us unprepared for the havoc it wrecked on our children and classrooms.

The rapid success of the Power Rangers reminds us of the need to remain ever vigilant for new multi-marketing phenomena which enter the early childhood popular culture, so that we are ready and able to play our rightful roles in counteracting their negative affects on children.

Reader Feedback

The ideas and experiences of teachers have provided the inspiration for this book. In the spirit of Peaceable Classrooms, I've included the question-naire below so that *your* thoughts can have a part in shaping what a Peaceable Classroom becomes. I welcome any ideas and experiences that you would like to share. Thank you.

-Diane

Were there specific classroom issues that led to your decision to purchase *Teaching Young Children in Violent Times*? If so, what were they?

What aspects of the book were most helpful to you?

Has the book had a direct impact on your classroom? If so, please describe.

(over)

Please provide an example(s) of how you used the book in your classroom.

Have you tried things in *your* work with young children that you think should be included in a book like this?

How might *Teaching Young Children in Violent Times* be improved to help adults better meet the needs of young children?

Is there anything else you would like me to know about your experience around this topic?

(optional):

name_____ phone_____

title_____

address_____

_____

Please describe your profession and/or work with young children:

Send your comments to Publications Director, ESR, 23 Garden Street, Cambridge, MA 02138.

About the Author

Diane Levin, Ph.D. is professor of education at Wheelock College in Boston, Massachusetts. For twenty five years, she has worked in teacher education and in a variety of early childhood classrooms. For the last twelve, her work has been inspired by co-raising her twelve year old son Eli.

Since 1982, Diane's research and writing have focused on how violence in society affects children. She has examined how media, toys, and popular culture influence children's social, political, and intellectual development and contribute to their socialization into a culture of violence. In recent years, her work has been centered increasingly on the wide range of ways violence enters children's lives. Throughout, Diane's goal has been to help parents and teachers gain a better understanding of how to raise healthier children, promote non-violence and conflict resolution, facilitate constructive and creative play, and break the cycle of violence in the lives of children and families.

Diane has served on the National Association for the Education of Young Children's Panel on Violence in the Lives of Children and Families. She has co-authored three other books with Nancy Carlsson-Paige: *Who's Calling the Shots?: How to Respond Effectively to Children's Fascination with War Play and War Toys* (New Society Publishers, Philadelphia), *The War Play Dilemma: Balancing Needs and Values in the Early Childhood Classroom* (Teachers College Press, New York), and *Helping Young Children Understand Peace, War, and the Nuclear Threat* (National Association for the Education of Young Children, Washington, D.C.).

About ESR

Educators for Social Responsibility seeks to make social responsibility an integral part of educaton in our nation's schools. We create and disseminate new ways of teaching and learning that help young people participate in shaping a better world.

Our programs and products present divergent viewpoints, stimulate critical thinking about controversial issues, teach creative and productive ways of dealing with differences, promote cooperative problem solving, and foster informed decision making. We help young people develop a personal commitment to the well-being of other people and the planet, and encourage participation in the democratic process.

ESR gratefully acknowledges the support of the William and Flora Hewlett Foundation, the Lippincott Foundation, the Scherman Foundation, the Sidney Stern Memorial Trust, and many dedicated, individual friends of ESR.

ESR Professional Development Workshops

"More than any other class, workshop, or in-service, this week has helped me grow as a person and as an educator."

— institute participant

ESR offers a wide range of training opportunities to meet the needs and budget of your school or organization. ESR programs match innovative ideas, age-appropriate classroom strategies, and the newest curricula in the field of teaching for social responsibiliity.

Our highly engaging workshops utilize a range of approaches from role plays and simulations to small-group discussions and reflective writing.

Training Formats to Fit Your Needs

Our formats include introductory workshops, one- to three-day seminars, in-service series, weeklong summer institutes and university courses, schoolbased model programs, consultation, and speakers on selected educational topics.

SCHOOL SERVICES IN CONFLICT RESOLUTION, VIOLENCE PREVENTION, AND INTERGROUP RELATIONS

ESR helps schools and school systems across the country set up comprehensive conflict resolution programs. Our goal is to help young people learn to deal with differences in healthy and productive ways.

ESR conflict resolution programs help educators provide effective instruction in conflict resolution on four levels:

1. incorporation into classroom management and approaches to displine

2. student skill instruction

3. infusion into subject areas

4. schoolwide initiatives

We provide:

- *introductory training program*

- *curricula and implementation manuals*

- *follow-up program*

- *leadership training opportunities*

Parent training and peer mediation programs are available.

Also Published by ESR

CONTINUING ON ESR'S BESTSELLER LIST
Elementary Perspective: Teaching Concepts of Peace and Conflicts

William J. Kreidler

This outstanding resource guide offers more than 80 activities that help teachers and students define peace, explore justice, and learn the value of conflict and its resolution. Designed to complement the standard curriculum, *Elementary Perspectives* engages students in thought-provoking activities that help them understand complex ideas such as prejudice, enemies, propaganda, and community.

Students read, write, draw, role-play, sing, and discuss their way through a process that helps them acquire the concrete cooperative and conflict resolution skills needed to become caring and socially responsible citizens.

Grades K-6
269 pages, ESR 1990
EPERS1
$28.00 Nonmembers,
$25.20 Members

Conflict Resolution in the Middle School: A Curriculum and Teaching Guide
DRAFT

William J. Kreidler

Middle school students are beginning to reexamine their relationships with peers, teachers, parents, and the world. *Conflict Resolution in the Middle School* presents over 150 activities to help students effectively handle the conflict that goes with this developmental stage.

Based on the unique needs of middle school students—and their teachers—the guide's ten basic skill areas teach students active listening, perspective taking, negotiation, and mediation. The activities are cooperatively structured and presented for three levels (grades six, seven, and eight). Through discussion, role plays, and journal writing, students broaden their definition of conflict, discover how conflicts escalate and de-escalate, and explore connections between diversity and conflicts.

Practical and innovative suggestions are offered for infusion into the standard middle school curriculum. Interdisciplinary teaching units are also provided.

Grades 6-8
196 pages, ESR 1994
CONMID
$25.00 Nonmembers
$22.50 Members

The Power of Numbers: A Teacher's Guide to Mathematics in a Social Studies Context

Fred Gross, Patrick Morton, and Rachel Poliner

The power of mathematics lies in its use as a tool not only for computing, but for making decisions, communicating, and predicting. This middle school math and social studies curriculum integrates goals and strategies, consistent with the National Council of Teachers of Mathematics *Standards*, to help students create mathematical questions; conduct research; record, interpret, and discuss results; and learn about the uses and misuses of math.

Using skills developed in middle and high school math, students work on thematic projects that require the use of many different math and reasoning skills. With the Census and polling as conecting threads, students explore high school dropout rates, the smoking and drinking habits of teenagers, the interpretation of crime statistics, and other interesting topics.

Grades 6-9
240 pages, ESR 1993
POWNUM
$35.00 Nonmembers
$31.50 Members

Unbound, student handout masters
POWPAC
$10.00 Nonmembers
$9.00 Members

Taking Part: An Elementary Curriculum in the Participation Series (Revised Edition)

Boston Area Eductors for Social Responsibility Sheldon Berman, series coordiantor

Taking Part offers lessons that help teach children how to make a difference in the classroom and in their everyday world. Activities explore many forms of democratic participation and empowerment, explain simple decision-making models, and introduce the electoral process.

Grade K-6
43 pages, ESR 1984, Revised 1991
TAKPAR
$19.00 Nonmembers
$17.10 Members

Trash Conflicts: A Science and Social Studies Curriculum on the Ethics of Disposal

Amy Ballin with Jeffrey Benson and Lucile Burt

Trash Conflicts promotes deeper understanding of the impact of waste production and disposal. It goes beyond awareness and increasing students' appreciation of natural resources to initiating critical thinking, decision making, responsibility, and empowerment. The curriculum starts where children are and moves them through a careful analysis of a complex series of interrelated issues, which include technology, economics, power, race, and class. It explores waste production and the impact of disposal methods from the personal to the community to the corporate.

Through science-based experiments, research and analysis, role plays, and discussions, students learn about the nature of garbage, disposal methods, consumer behavior, toxic waste, and the political process surrounding trash disposal. They investigate the links between waste management and issues of race and class, creating new ways to consider environmental responsibility.

Grades 6-8
220 pages, ESR 1993
TRASHD
$25.00 Nonmembers
$22.50 Members

Dealing with Differences: Conflict Resolution in Our Schools

Dealing with Differences has received praise from hundreds of teachers, administrators, and community leaders. This booklet presents ESR's unique and highly successful approach to creative conflict resolution.

ESR's approach is student-centered and emphasizes conflict as a normal part of life; as such, conflict presents opportunities for growth. Through inquiry into and exploration of the underlying issues (including individual, racial, and ethnic differences, and prejudice), students begin to understand the complex factors that lead to conflict.

Our approach entails a comprehensive program that includes classroom management, skill enhancement, and curriculum infusion that increases students' ability to fashion "win-win" solutions and creatively resolve conflicts.

13 pages, ESR 1991
Single copy
DEAL01
$1.75

Packet of 10
DEAL02
$10.00

Secrecy and Democracy

Steven Cohen

Through a variety of readings and activities, *Secrecy and Democracy* explores covert action in the United States government and raises complex questions about the role of secrecy in a democratic society. Using the history of covert acton from the creation of the CIA to the Iran/contra affair, students consider conflict between national security and open government, learn about the growth of the national security state, and examine the consequences on the American system of checks and balances on the free press.

Produced in collaboration with the Tufts University Experimental College Symposia Project, directed by Sherman Teichman.

High School/College
140 pages, ESR 1990
SECREC
Nonmembers $11.25
Members $10.15

Making History:
A Social Studies Curriculum
in the Participation Series

Boston Area Educators for Social Responsibility
Sheldon Berman, series coordinator

Making History helps teachers prepare students for democratic participation in society. Students are encouraged to use their own experiences to assess controversial issues. Activities explore the meaning of empowerment, both in the community and in the nation at large. Students review case studies of community action, learn about various models for decision making, and discuss strategies for creating change.

Grades 7-12
90 pages, ESR 1984
MAKHIS
$19.00 Nonmembers,
$17.10 Members

ESR Journal:
Educating for Democracy

The ESR Journal continues to offer K-12 and postsecondary educators practical strategies and great ides for making social responsibility a reality in the classroom and in children's lives.

The ESR Journal is a reservoir of resources on promising practices in the field of education for social responsibility, highlighting *what works* and *why*.

106 pages, ESR 1992
JOUR02
$13.00 Nonmembers,
$11.70 Members

ESR Journal:
Educating for Social
Responsibility

The first edition of the *ESR Journal* offers an exciting array of essays outlining theoretical and practical strategies for educating for social responsibility. Volume one contains offerings from leading educators throughout the country, including Vito Perrone (director of Harvard's Teacher Education Program), William J. Kreidler (author of *Creative Conflict Resolution*), and Sam Totten (University of Arkansas).

121 pages, ESR 1990
JOUR01
$13.00 Nonmembers,
$11.70 Members

VIDEOS!

Everybody Rejoice:
A Celebration of Diversity

29th Street Video Production/ESR

This video adds a new and engaging dimension to school conflict resolution and multicultural/diversity programs. An ethnically diverse group of high school students from the Public School Repertory Company present a collage of performances and perspectives that pay tribute to their individual and ethnic differences.

An uplifting, entertaining experience as well as an effective demonstration of how working together toward a common goal can positively effect students' sense of self, their awareness and appreciation of diversity and individuality, and their efficacy as members of a community working toward a common goal.

Video comes with a two-page users' guide complete with pre- and post-viewing discussion questions. Produced by Tony De Nonno; coproduced by David Wallace

**High School
26-minute videotape (1/2 VHS),
ESR 1991
EVBODY
$25.00 Nonmembers,
$22.50 Members**

Interested in starting a school conflict resolution program?

This series of videos from the Resolving Conflict Creatively Program (RCCP) offers moving testimonies and vivid snapshots of what conflict resolution can look like in your school.

RCCP is a collaborative effort of the New York City Public Schools and Educators for Social Responsibility Metropolitan Area. One of the most successful programs in the nation, it promotes effective instruction in creative conflict resolution and intergroup relations. (Videos include contact information for the RCCP program.)

Waging Peace in Our Schools

This moving video offers you a chance to experience the in-depth components of the RCCP. You'll see conflict resolution skills being taught and students engaged in a peer mediation, as well as hear the testimonies of children, teachers, parents, and administrators who have worked to change their schools. Dramatic positive changes are possible when an entire school community wages peace. Produced by Peter Barton. (26 minutes) **WAGEPE**

**$39.95 Nonmembers
$35.95 Members**

A Fistful of Words

(Adult version) This video describes the main components of the RCCP. Teachers, principals, students, and local school board members share their enthusiasm about making conflict resolution a regular part of the school curriculum. Produced by Tony De Nonno. (23 minutes) **FISTAD**

(Student version) Focusing on one component of the RCCP—mediation—students share how they feel about being peer mediators and role-play the steps involved in mediation. Includes a two-page user's guide. Produced by Tony De Nonno. Grades 3-12. (13 minutes) **FISTST**

Making a Difference

This video highlights the dramatic changes in attitudes and behaviors of teachers and students in the RCCP in relation to dealing with conflict. Produced by Linda Lantieri. 5th grade-Adult. (26 minutes) **MAKDIF**

An Eye for an Eye...
Makes the Whole World Blind

Alternative high school students, teachers, and their principal share the dramatic changes they have experienced in attitudes and behaviors in dealing with conflict in their lives, changes brought about as a result of their participation in the RCCP. Produced by Peter Barton. Grades 7-12. (12 minutes) **EYE-FOR**

$25.00 Nonmembers,
$22.50 Members each video

Customer Service

We guarantee your satisfaction. Call our friendly customer service representative for helpful responses to your questions and to order products and services.

How to Order...

By phone—use our TOLL-FREE-NUMBER. Simply call 1-800-370-2515, 9am-5pm EST

By fax—fax your order in by calling 617-864-5164 (include your credit card number or purchase order)

By mail—send your order form to: ESR, 23 Garden Street, Suite 104, Cambridge, MA 02138

RUSH ORDER—call our toll-free number or fax your order. We'll get your materials to you within seven days—GUARANTEED. ($5 handling charge on rush order)

Shipping and handling

Add 10% of total ($2.50 minimum) in U.S. and Canada; add 20% of total ($4.50 minimum) outside U.S. and Canada. Please allow 2-4 weeks for delivery. Rush order available; see order form. Prices may be subject to change. Refund policy: Full refund if items are returned within 30 days in saleable condition.

Pay by...

Credit card—MasterCard or Visa
Check—*made payable to ESR*
Purchase order

VOLUME DISCOUNTS—

We offer volume discounts when you order:

5-49 copies of a product - 10%

50+ copies of a product - 15%

SATISFACTION GUARANTEED

If not completely satisfied with an ESR product, simply return it within 30 days in saleable condition for a full refund.

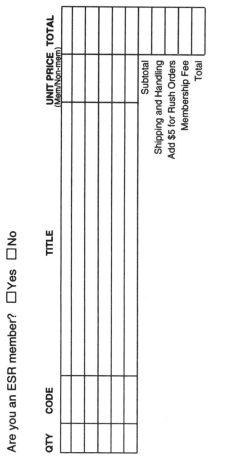

Order Form

☐ Enclosed is my check or money order in US funds.
☐ Enclosed is a purchase order.
☐ Charge my order to: ☐ MasterCard ☐ Visa
Card # _____ Exp. date _____
Signature _____
Phone _____

Bill to:
Street Address
City, State, Zip

Ship to:
Street Address*
City, State, Zip
*Use street address for UPS delivery

Mail all orders to: Sales Manager, ESR, 23 Garden Street, Cambridge, MA 02138
1-800-370-2515

Are you an ESR member? ☐ Yes ☐ No

QTY	CODE	TITLE	UNIT PRICE (Mem/Non-mem)	TOTAL
			Subtotal	
			Shipping and Handling	
			Add $5 for Rush Orders	
			Membership Fee	
			Total	